Sea Glass House Murder

A Beach Girls Mystery

Susan Bridges Winters

Sea Glass House Murder

This novel is dedicated to my mother in heaven, Betty Bridges, and my father, Bobby Bridges, who showed me that reading can be enjoyable and instilled in me a love for the public library and reading.

Table of Contents

1

Chapter One

September 9th, 2021, marked the beginning of the Beach Girls' fourteenth year of beach vacations together. We started out as high school friends and are now family. The ladies have gone through divorces, deaths, and raising children. Some are now helping to raise grandchildren. Many of us are caring for our elderly mothers and fathers, taking them to their doctor appointments and cooking their meals. I guess one could say that we are surviving womanhood. We are kind, loving women. However, we are very intuitive and adventurous, and those attributes are what really join us together.

"The Beach Girls" is what we call ourselves. We are six 57-year-old high school friends who still act like teenagers when we get together. We graduated from an urban high school of twenty-four hundred students. Of those, there were six hundred seniors in our class. In our early forties, after our twenty-year class reunion, a group of female classmates started having dinner together once a month at various restaurants in

Jacksonville. Initially, we were twenty-four female classmates. Since that time, we have lost dear friends. The six of us became very close at those dinners and decided to take a beach vacation together. At first, I wasn't sure we could all stay in one house together with our different personalities. However, the trip was successful, and that is why our little group is known as the Beach Girls. It was at our first beach vacation the six of us bonded as sisters.

My name is Sara, and I am an English teacher at West Ryder High School in a small country town in north Florida, just outside of Jacksonville. In my town, everybody knows your children and has no problem calling you when the kids do something wrong. We have one grocery store, Winn Dixie, and six fast-food restaurants. The nearest city is Jacksonville and that is where the Beach Girls spend their time shopping and dining out. Everyone in my little town attends the high school's Friday night football game; it is a community event. The high school's parking lot is filled with trucks and SUVs. We have a small Christmas Parade each year, and the main road through town is closed until after the parade.

I live on the outskirts of the county on five acres. I have a small, three-bedroom brick house with an in-ground swimming pool and a pond in my front yard. Each day I get to see bunnies, squirrels, and all sorts of birds. It is not a farm, far from being one, yet I have a small, waist-high wooden box garden, a plethora of lizards, and one dog, Sweetie. My grandkids and I found Sweetie at the Dog Pound, rescued her, and brought her home to live with Weston and me.

I was married at twenty and worked while my ex-husband went to law school. I have a real estate license, a paralegal degree, and a bachelor's degree in English and Reading. I have a wonderful son, Michael, who owns a sporting goods company and is doing rather well. My sweet, lovely daughter-in-law, Cynthia, handles all the merchandize for cheerleaders. They have three children, who are my heart: Brooks, Rylan, and Caroline. Brooks and Rylan play baseball and football for their schools and travel teams. Caroline likes to ride horses, English style, and play tennis. She just started piano lessons and told me she knows two songs already. I inform Caroline that she is her daddy's mini-me. They are a busy family and often go out of town during baseball season. I am currently remarried to a great man named Weston, who is a business agent for the local Thirteen Frost and Refrigeration Union in Jacksonville. Why this is important, you will soon learn.

Weston and I like our privacy and pretty much stay to ourselves. I have my sisters and brother, the Beach Girls, and teachers at my school for company, while Weston has a few buddies from high school and work.

The Beach Girls group includes: Lizzy, a five-foot-four-inches brunette with a great smile and brown eyes; Mary Beth, a five-foot-three-inches blond with golden highlights, blue eyes, and big boobs; Cecilia or Cici, a five-foot-seven-inches nature girl with wild, white and gray, curly hair, blue eyes, and beautiful brown skin. Nancy is five feet 6 inches tall, with reddish brown hair and blue eyes. She is a very smart lady. Then, there is Elle, for Elizabeth. She is a five-foot-eleven-inches tall woman with long legs, short, reddish-blond hair, and green eyes. She is also pretty.

Lastly, there is me, a five-foot-four-inches brunette with caramel streaks placed randomly in my hair, crystal blue eyes, and olive skin. Sometimes, I have red hair or even silver/purple hair. I am the "cross the line" type of woman and love to get into mischief with my girls. I love sports and am a risk-taker; life is too short. Sometimes, I can't hold my tongue and it gets me into trouble.

Lizzy, a widow, owns a concrete company and has many contacts on the East Coast. Her husband, Mitchell, died a couple of years ago in a car accident; a drunk driver in a semi-truck hit his SUV head-on. That year was a very sad one for all of us. I called him "Mitchie," and he was like a brother to me. Lizzy is a strong-willed woman who also runs a farm in rural Macclenny, Florida, where she raises cattle and chickens. Lizzy has "barn cats," as she calls them, and gives each one a name. She also has a huge black bull named "Dub." One day, while at Lizzy's farm, I was wearing black pants and was bent over getting something out of my car when Dub came running toward me. I was lucky there was a fence between Dub and me; I think he thought I was his girlfriend. He is the stud of the pasture.

Mary Beth works for the United States Postal Service in Jacksonville, Florida, and is a divorcee with two children. Lexi, a.k.a Snoop Dog, is Mary Beth's daughter and is married to a Flagler County policeman, Jason. They sometimes help us out with our investigations. Snoop Dog normally works as a veterinarian at their local dog pound. She usually takes home one of the dogs at night to make sure they are getting the right meds. Snoop Dog and Jason have four dogs of their own: a German shepherd, a terrier, a hound, and a teacup poodle.

Cici is a nurse at Methodist General Hospital and is the "mother nature" of the group. She loves the outdoors and growing her own fruits and vegetables. She is always trying to get the Beach Girls to eat healthier. Cici works in the emergency room and is full of funny stories. The way she pronounces some of her words is in the true southern manner, but delightful. She is truly a one of a kind lady.

Nancy works for the DEA in New York as an agent. She is married, and her husband works for the Federal Bureau of Investigation. She moved to New York after high school, met a nice man, and married him. Nancy is the calm one of the group. She tells us she is still a southern girl even if she lives in New York City. Nancy doesn't drink alcohol, but she is not against any of us drinking when we are all together.

Elle works for the City of Jacksonville and is married. Her husband's name is Ryan. Her husband is also a retired veteran and loves to hunt deer and be outdoors. At one time, he worked with the IRS as an accountant. Elle is a whiz at the computer; it is amazing the amount of information that girl can find out. She is also very observant and smart. Elle lives in a small country town at the state border next to Georgia.

Chapter Two

Last September, while still at the Tybee Island beach house, we decided to pick a new location for our upcoming beach vacation. The Beach Girls have been going to Tybee Island, Georgia, for the past five years. We have dined in all of Savannah's finest restaurants. Mrs. Randall's Boarding House is one of our favorites. Lizzy suggests going back to St. Augustine or the Marineland area in Florida, which is closer to almost all of us. Other than Nancy, we all live in northeast Florida and agree that the short ride would be great.

"Let's look for places in St. Augustine or Crescent Beach in Flagler County," Lizzy quickly responds. "I can look up some beach houses on the internet and see what kind of prices they have," she adds.

"Matanzas has a lot of places we can rent, and some are pretty isolated right on the beach," chimes in Mary Beth. "My sister, Betty Ann, and my family rented a five bedroom and four baths house right on the ocean with a beautiful ocean view. We had to share a pool with a couple of other houses, but no one seemed to mind," Mary Beth adds. "It was so relaxing and everyone had plenty of room. The place was so nice," she finishes.

"I'm in," I say.

"I'm in," replies Nancy.

"I'm down!" yells Cici from the kitchen.

"Count me in," adds Lizzy.

The decision was made, Lizzy and Mary Beth got busy taking notes of "must haves" for our next beach house. "We 'must have' at least three bathrooms," says Mary Beth.

"We must have at least six full or three queen-size beds," says Nancy.

"We must have a swimming pool," says Elle.

"We must be next to the ocean with full ocean views," says Lizzy.

"We must have a big kitchen," I say.

Lizzy and Mary Beth usually set up the reservations for our house at the beach as they both like researching on the internet. When it comes to things like that, I leave it up to someone else and go with the flow. Besides, I have to get back to the classroom and prepare my students for the FSA Reading test. The Florida State Assessment is a test that all Florida students must pass to graduate high school. That is a lot of pressure for me and other teachers, not to mention the poor students.

A month later, we all receive a text from Lizzy on our cell phones. "Attached is a list of three beach houses in Matanzas Inlet with three bedrooms each. Two of the houses have two queen beds each, and one has a king bed. The houses have four bathrooms, a huge deck, and swimming pools. And yes, they are right on the beach with direct ocean views. One is located with the Atlantic Ocean in front and the Matanzas Inlet at the back, but it has an above-ground pool with a large deck. Take a look at the pictures and let us know your selection. The top vote count gets our pick. Have a great day, girls."

After viewing the houses on the internet and checking out the locations, I chose the Sea Glass House, a two-story house located between the Atlantic Ocean, in front, and the Matanzas Inlet, behind the house. The views from the house were amazing; white, sandy beaches and emerald waves of salt water splashing onto the shore. Thankfully, the other ladies decide on the same house. We are all set for our next beach vacation at the Matanzas Inlet.

Lizzy, Mary Beth, and I take a Saturday the next month and drive down to Matanzas to look at the Sea Glass House. We take Lizzy's car and drive down AIA turning onto the road to the house. We drive down the bumpy, overused road and arrive at the house. The location could not be more beautiful. We get out of Lizzy's car and face the Atlantic Ocean. The sun is shining, and it looks like diamonds are floating along the ocean waves. The color of the water is greenish-blue, and the white foamat the top of the waves drops slowly into the moving water as the waves rush to the shoreline.

"Oh my, this is lovely. Look at that water," says Lizzy.

"Wow, I am glad we picked this house," says Mary Beth. She pulls out her cell phone to take pictures. "I am going to send these photos to the other girls," she adds.

"Let's walk around to the Matanzas Inlet side," I say.

Just next to the side of the house is an above-ground pool. The owners have built wooden stairs and a wooden deck around the pool, just large enough for lounge chairs and small tables. The pool must be at least twenty-five feet long and fifteen feet wide. It has two ladders leading down into the fresh, clear water. The pool will be perfect to swim and wash off before going into the house after a relaxing day on the beach. A hose attached to the water spigot is curled up like a black snake. I jump back and laugh when Mary Beth squeals.

We walk toward the back of the house, which is high on stilts. The view was amazing too. A small dock, thirty-five feet long, appears to float in the blue, salt water. Tiki torches line their way along the L-shaped walkway. A small area at the end of the dock is roped off for kayaks and canoes. The water in the inlet is bluer than the ocean and more serene. There are a couple of kayaks out on the water as the boaters gently glide across the smooth, liquid surface. "Cici will love this dock. You know she will bring a canoe or float," I say.

We return to the front of the house and climb the stairs to the large, wrap-around porch. Lizzy has the door code, and we enter the house. We look at all the bedrooms and baths as well as the kitchen. "Look, they have an extra ice maker; we won't have to go to the minute market for ice every day. The girls are going to love this place. I think we found our new beach home," says Lizzy.

"I am taking a picture of the living room and kitchen and sending it to the girls," says Mary Beth. She pulls her cell out of her purse, takes a few shots of the house, and texts the photos to the other Beach Girls.

A few moments after, Mary Beth adds, "Cici and Elle have already texted the thumbs-up emoji."

"You two did a great job finding this house. Thank you for all your hard work; it has paid off for all of us," I say, knowing that Mary Beth and Lizzy have spent many hours looking for houses that would please all of us.

"I can't wait," says Mary Beth.

Chapter Three

The following months fly by with Thanksgiving and Christmas. For Christmas, my son rents a large mountain cabin in the Blue Ridge Mountains in a town called Jackson Hll, North Carolina. The first morning, snow falls, covering the mountaintops with a white blanket. That day, we go skiing with the grandkids and have a wonderful time skiing and sledding down a nearby ski slope at the Mountaintop Ski Resort.

There is a great restaurant named The Davy Crockett Inn, built on the top of a mountain in a small settlement. The inn doesn't have any bedrooms anymore, as they have all converted into individual dining areas with vintage country decor. Each room has a plethora of antiques hanging on the walls and pictures of frontier men and women. All the furniture in the inn is made of rustic pine and oak wood. The eatery makes one think of the people who traveled out west to settle on the plains. These men and women created this small town with their hand saws and a few tools. The restaurant serves its food in large bowls, old family style, and they serve the best comfort food. So, even if one is feeling down in the dumps, they can't help but feel warm and cozy after eating one of the Davy Crockett meals. Our family visits twice for dinner while we are in the mountains. The grandkids love their apple fritters and fried chicken. I like the chicken and dumplings. Weston and Michael like the fried pork chops and mashed potatoes with brown gravy. Cynthia enjoys the baked apples and cherry pie.

We all had a wonderful time that week with everlasting, cherishable memories of each other. The kids go skiing, mining, tubing, and hiking. Weston and I mined a few amethysts and had a jeweler in the town cut them in diamond shapes. I plan to make a couple of rings with them

The grandchildren even find a baby squirrel that has fallen from an old pine tree. Michael, Cynthia, and the kids take it to the veterinarian, but they have to leave the squirrel with the vet since we will go home tomorrow. Caroline is not happy; she has given the squirrel a name, Buddy.

For New Year's Eve, the Beach Girls, Weston, Ryan, Elle's husband, and I drive to Amelia Island for dinner and fireworks at Vinnie's Italian restaurant located right on the pier. They serve the best cannoli and fettuccine alfredo with grilled chicken. At midnight, we toast the New Year with our champagne glasses and watch from the beach as the Ritz Carlton shoots off a multitude of fireworks. My favorite firework is the red, white, and blue flares. As I watch them fall to the white beach, I think of Cici's son, who is in the military. I feel a rush of pride for all the soldiers who died for our country.

"What are you doing?" I ask Cici as she waves a sparkler around her head.

"I am lighting up for the new year," she says as a spark lands on the sleeve of her red jacket, which immediately catches fire. Weston grabs her around her waist and throws Cici down on the sand, rolling her back and forth to get the fire out.

"Stop slapping me!" yells Weston. "You're on fire!" he adds.

"Sorry," replies Cici in a whimpering voice.

Weston pulls Cici up from the sandy beach as I walk over to her side. "Guess you light up New Year's after all," I said

All the others joined in, "Light her up! Light her up!" We all had a good laugh, including Cici. Luckily she was safe and had only a small burn hole in her red jacket.

Chapter Four

It's finally St. Patrick's Day; eighty degrees, a perfect spring day for Florida. Lizzy, Mary Beth, Elle, and I are sitting in McGintey's Tavern at a table in the back near an old wooden bar. The place is decorated with green cloverleaves, green and white balloons, and green streamers hanging from the ceiling. An Irishman is standing on a small stage playing his bagpipes, and two of the waitresses are dancing a jig in celebration of the day. Several Irishmen with red hair and long beards, wearing kilts are toasting one another with their Guinness beers over at the bar.

Mary Beth is wearing a silk, green blouse with a green and black kilt over dark green tights and black leather boots. Lizzy and Elle have black jeans and green tee shirts on, embroidered with "Kiss me I'm Irish" across their chests. I am wearing my St. Patrick's Day dress of Kelly green with tiny white embroidered four-leaf clovers. It is too hot for me to wear tights or jeans. I am also wearing my small, green hat with two large, four-leaf clovers springing from the top. I look like a big elf. St. Patrick's Day is special to us as we have Irish blood in our DNA according to the tests we all mailed in to get our ancestry connections.

All of a sudden, Cici enters the restaurant wearing a tight, Kelly green fitness getup and waiving her hands around. "Where's the restroom! Where's the restroom!" she yells. She looks even stranger in the skin-tight leotard; I don't look that much like an elf, after all. I point to the restroom door.

"What's going on with her?" I ask as she jogs past the table.

"I have no idea," says Elle shaking her head in disbelief.

A few minutes later, Cici arrives at the table and sits next to Lizzy. The waitress comes to the table at the same time and takes our drink order of a pitcher of Guinness and five glasses.

"Cici, what is going on with you?" I ask.

"Well, y'all are not going to believe what has just happened to me on my way over to McKintey's. I was driving down Jamison Drive when I had to stop at the red light on the corner of Jamison and Reddick Drive. The elementary school was letting the kids out and the crossing guard was getting ready to let the students cross. I looked out the passenger side window and saw this old, gray-haired man with a long beard taking off his pants. I pull the SUV off the road, jump out of the car, and grab a blanket I keep for emergencies out of the back of the car. I stood next to the old man holding up the blanket so the kids couldn't see his old butt. I yell, 'What are you doing?!'

By this time, he was bare-ass naked. 'I have to sheeet,' he said, pulling all of his clothes off.

'Put your clothes back on. There are little kids trying to cross the road!' I yelled, standing there still holding up the blanket with the red hearts. I glanced over to the crossing guard to make sure the kids were not seeing this crazy old coot.

The crossing guard had seen what was happening and ushered the students back across Reddick toward the school. I noticed her pulling out her cell and realized she was calling the police. I looked back over to the old man; he was running into the woods with his pants and underwear hanging from his old, dirty hands. He had finished 'sheeting' and ran. A few minutes later, the police arrived, and I explained what had happened. That was the last I saw of the man and the police. I could still smell that stinking 'sheeet'," says Cici.

The men at the bar overhear Cici's story and try not to laugh by covering their mouths, but that doesn't work. They all burst out laughing. I can't help myself either, so I start laughing too. Soon all the girls are laughing. Cici, smiling, says, "His old pecker was all wrinkled up, just like his old face." We all laugh some more. The men enjoy Cici's story so much that they buy her another pitcher of beer.

"I think you deserve this after your drive over," says one of the bearded men.

Chapter Five

Easter arrives and is filled with family attending the Easter service at Exchange Church, not too far from my house. My entire family is at the service, including Pop. After the service, the family travels to our house for Easter dinner.

The other Beach Girls spend the day with their families, attending church, having dinner, and hiding eggs for the Easter egg hunt.

This year Weston sets up a couple of large tents on the front lawn for the family to dine under, and I set up a buffet table for the food. I bake ham and turkey while the other family members bring their favorite dishes. My sister, Barbara, cooks a rice and broccoli casserole that is divine and a sweet potato soufflé covered with pecan bits and brown sugar. Cynthia, my daughter-in-law, makes a dish of fresh carrots, green beans wrapped in bacon, and roasted red potatoes.

After lunch, all the adults hide the Easter eggs as the kids wait inside the house. While walking around the front yard, I glance back toward the house and see Caroline peeking through the blinds in my bedroom window. I point at her; she laughs and closes the blinds. I know that little girl is watching from somewhere. She, too, has an inquisitive mind. The grandkids and cousins find their eggs, after which we eat dessert. I made two pumpkin rolls with caramel icing and white cupcakes with green coconut icing with jellybeans placed on top. The cupcakes look like tiny Easter baskets. Barbara made a delicious trifold of fresh fruit: strawberries, blueberries, and blackberries. I sleep by eight; Weston is next to me in bed, snoring.

Chapter Six

At the beginning of May, Lizzy texts the Beach Girls, "Jason just called; they are doing two-for-one massages at the Ritz Carlton at Amelia Island. How many of you want to go? We can split the fees."

"I want a massage," I text.

"Count me in," texts Mary Beth

"I'll take a day off for that," texts Elle.

"I can't make it; I have to work. Covid has still got us working overtime; the ICU is full of Covid patients," says Cici.

"I will set the massage appointments for Saturday, May 4th, so you ladies won't have to take time off from work," texts Lizzy.

Saturday, May 4th, arrives, and we meet at the Circle K station in Yulee.

"I'll drive; everyone can ride with me," I say. "Your cars will be secure here at the station. They have a full-time security guard," I add.

"Great," says Lizzy.

"Okay," says Mary Beth.

"Works for me," says Elle.

"Make sure you have your face masks with you," I say.

We arrive at the Ritz, and Jason meets us in the lobby. "Good morning, beautiful ladies," he says.

We all give Jason a big group hug. "Hey baby," says Lizzy as she cuddles her son. Sons and daughters are never too old for a mom to love. I do the same with Michael.

"I will escort you ladies to the salon, and then the massage therapists will take you to your rooms. We have booked you in rooms for two; Mom and Miss Sara in one and Miss Mary Beth and Miss Elle in the other," says Jason.

Once on the salon floor, the therapists lead us to our respective rooms. We remove our clothes and wrap a sheet around our bodies. After thirty minutes or so, I hear a ruckus in the room next to us. Apparently, Elle is having an allergic reaction to the sea scrub lotion her massage therapist is using.

"My lips are swelling!" she yells.

"Oh my goodness, you look like a blowfish!" screams Mary Beth.

"Did you touch your lips?" asks the therapist, moving to the top of the massage bed to look at Elle.

"It smells so good; I rubbed some on my fingers so I could smell the scent. It must have touched my lips," says Elle through swollen lips.

"Calm down; I have some medication for allergies in my storage cabinet. I have seen this before and can help you," says the therapist in a calming, sweet voice.

"Hurry up before her lips explode!" yells Mary Beth staring at Elle's lips. Her lips are getting bigger and bigger.

Back in the other room, Lizzy and I wrap our sheets around our naked bodies and jump from the massage table. We run into the room next door, holding onto our sheets. "Wow, is your tongue swollen too?" I ask, worried that she may stop breathing.

Elle shakes her head back and forth to indicate a no.

"Is there shellfish in the lotion?" asks Lizzy.

Elle shakes her head again.

Meanwhile, Mary Beth says, "I don't know, but I have got to take a picture of those lips. I wonder if I could put some lipstick on them."

Elle tries to grab Mary Beth by the arm, but she gets away, pulls her cell phone out of her bag, and snaps a few pictures. I am sure Mary Beth will send Nancy and Cici the pictures. I notice Elle's eyes start to bulge.

Just then, Jason comes into the room with the medication. "I heard Elle had a reaction to the sea scrub lotion. I have a cure right here," he says, holding up a medicine tube. "Miss Elle, just think, you won't have to get cosmetic surgery to inflate your lips. You can just buy some sea scrub from us and use it before you go out," he says, smiling and gently rubbing the medication on her lips.

"Jason, did that scrub have shrimp shells in it?" asks Lizzy.

"Yes, it does. Is that what Miss Elle is allergic to?" asks Jason as he rubs in the medication.

Elle whispers through her swollen lips, "Yes."

"You are not supposed to eat it, Miss Elle," says Jason as he tenderly rubs Elle's puffy lips.

After a few minutes, Elle's lips are back to normal, and we go back next door for the remainder of our massages. Mary Beth holds on to her camera as Elle keeps trying to grab it from her.

We complete our massages and catch the elevator to the Salt Bar Restaurant for lunch. This quaint restaurant is wonderful; the salt bar contains a variety of salt flavors that are used to cook the meals. We order small slices of ribeye and pick out our salt flavor. The chef melts the salt with butter and then pours the liquid over the steak as it is grilled on an open fire. The aroma of the salt and steak fills the room, inciting our taste buds. The flavors are delicious, and the steak is so tender it can be cut with butter knives. I wish the other girls could be here: Cici and Nancy are missing out on a treat.

Chapter Seven

At the end of May, Weston and I take my father, Pop, out to Gulf Port and Biloxi, Mississippi, for a little gambling. Pop is a good-looking, 88-year-old widower with five children, three of which are over 65 and on social security, eight grandchildren, and eight great-grandchildren, with the ninth on the way. He lives in his house in St. Augustine, still drives his Chevy extended cab truck, and plants a big garden on my sister's farm. Barbara has a forty-acre farm in the countryside of our town. Pop likes to gamble, and I am the fruit of the old tree.

Weston, Pop, and I load the SUV with our luggage and snacks and head west on I-10 for the Island View Casino and Hotel in Gulfport, MS. Since Pop is a high-stakes gambler, we get free rooms at the Island View. The trip takes us six hours with a stop at the Cracker Barrel, Pop's favorite country restaurant in Tallahassee because of all the delicious southern veggies and cornbread. They have the best turnip greens and pork necks in the state of Florida. The building includes a large shopping area. I shop around their store and purchase a pretty denim dress that will look good with my calf-high, brown leather boots. I pay for my dress and pick up a pink fairy bookmark for Caroline and some beef jerky for Brooks and Rylan. Afterward, we get back into the SUV and head west on I-10.

"I love this rest stop," I say to Pop as we walk around the hilltop, looking at the birds and squirrels. "It is always so beautiful out here with the animals and tall pine trees," I add.

"Yeah, I remember stopping here and sleeping for a few hours when I would drive out to Biloxi to gamble for a night," he says. "You can't do that today," he adds.

"Are y'all ready to get back on the road," says Weston coming up behind us.

"Let's do it," says Pop.

Once we get to the Island View, the valet removes our luggage and parks the car. Pop tips him a twenty, and off we go to check-in. The Island View is twelve stories high, with a double tower hotel. One of the towers sits directly on the beach. We stay in the beach tower overlooking the Gulf of Mexico. The turquoise-color ocean looks beautiful, with very few waves to be seen. The sand is as white as the columns on Jefferson's plantation house down the road.

The hotel also includes a non-smoking casino with large windows that have full ocean views. This tower has access to a pool and the gulf shores. We check into Suite 4220, set the luggage down in the large, airy room, and have the valet bring the SUV back around. Now is the time to hit the casinos in Biloxi, a short drive east up the coast.

The drive from Gulf Port to Biloxi takes only a few minutes. We drive along the coast and watch the people walk barefoot along the shore, struggling against the wind. I look out my window and see a seagull fighting a fierce wind, trying to fly down the shoreline. We pass Thomas Jefferson's house and notice it is open to the public. "One day, when we visit, I want to visit the Thomas Jefferson house," I say. I have said that on numerous occasions; I hope to someday.

"We can do that," says Pop. "I haven't been there either," he adds.

First stop, the Beaurivage Casino. We park the SUV on the third floor of the self-parking lot, enter the elevator, and make our way to the hotel lobby on the first floor. "Remember, we are on the third floor," I say. As in most casinos, the walkway to the casino contains a variety of shops, delis, coffee vendors, and a variety of bling to purchase in the stores before you lose your money and on your way out of the casino so that you can spend your winnings. This hotel has the most beautiful, colorful, live flower arrangements placed into huge ceramic vases on ornate tables of gold. There are numerous table settings spread throughout the building. The place is immaculate; no trash anywhere, not even a speck of dust.

The place is so clean one could probably eat off their floor; the bathrooms are well attended also. I feel safe here, especially with Covid spreading. Of course, we have already gotten our Covid vaccines and are wearing our masks. I wash my hands often to be sure I don't catch the virus. It is so sad that seven hundred thousand plus American people have already died from that vicious ever-morphing virus.

Pop and Weston win a lot more than I do. Perhaps this will be my lucky weekend. As we walk into the beautifully decorated casino, an array of photos of the latest winners hang in the air to excite new gamblers into laying out their money. I take a look at the hanging photos and don't recognize anyone. I know I sound negative, but don't get me wrong, I get all tingly inside when I see the bright lights and hear the hypnotizing sounds coming from the slot machines. Fun times are waiting for me at the slots. Weston likes to play at poker machines and drink. Beer and Bloody Mary are his choices of drinks. Pop is a Coca-Cola and coffee man. He plays cards at the tables and usually wins big in three-card poker.

I need to get a new club card to get points for playing and a free room or food. I walk over to the player's club window and give the lady my driver's license. She welcomes me to the casino and hands me a new card.

Afterward, I walk over to the slot machines with all the bright lights and noise; the hair on my arms is standing straight up. My favorite slot machines are the ones where people get to slap or move their hands across the screen. Today, I am playing the "Slap the Sharks" game. I put a hundred dollar bill into the machine, wait until the money is recorded, and push the play button. After a few tries, I hit a "Slap the Sharks". I slap twelve sharks on the screen and win five hundred dollars. I do a little jig! A few people have gathered around laughing as I stand and slap with both hands. I really get animated when I play these games, arms flaying and hands slapping at the screen. Needless to say, I don't win enough to get my picture taken, but who cares. Five hundred dollars means I keep playing the slots.

Pop, Weston, and I meet for dinner a few hours later. I find Weston playing poker on one of the machines at the Ocean Waves Bar and sit next to him. A few minutes later, Pop comes around the half-wall to the bar. "Y'all ready to eat?" he asks.

"Yes, I am hungry," says Weston drinking his last sip of a Bloody Mary.

We walk down the corridor to the elevator and press the button to the third floor. Once on the third floor, we leave the elevator and head to the SUV.

"I'll drive."

Pop gets into the front seat, and Weston opens the door to the back seat. We decide to go to a nice seafood restaurant called "Slap Yo Momma." The chef is known as the best chef in Biloxi; at one time, he worked in Emeril's restaurant in New Orleans. The food is amazing: fried shrimp, jambalaya, scallops, sea bass, oysters, and the best collard greens in the south. The chef uses a special seasoning made in New Orleans. I happen to walk by the kitchen on my way to the restroom and see a Jack's Creole seasoning container on the counter next to the grill. Yes, I will pick up some from a nearby grocery store before we go home.

"I won five hundred on the "Slap the Sharks" game," I announce proudly.

Weston responds with, "I didn't lose anything, so I guess I am even."

Pop quietly says, "I'm up thirteen hundred."

I say, "You buy dinner."

"No problem," Pop smiles as he responds. We all laugh; I love that man.

We stay at the Island View Hotel and Casino and travel back and forth to Biloxi for three days. We visit every casino in the twenty-mile radius; there are quite a few. I only lose two hundred of my five hundred dollars. Boy, did I have a blast with that money! Weston and I never lose more than a couple hundred a piece; we call it our play money. On the other hand, Pop wins big this time which is normal for him. We never know how much he finally wins, but let's just say that Pop usually has enough points to pay for all the meals while we are there. The casinos keep sending him free nights, hoping to get some of their money back.

Chapter Eight

September arrives, and the Beach Girls get ready to head to the beach. Lizzy, Mary Beth, and I drive down together. We meet at my house and load the SUV with everything baring the kitchen sink, and head down to Matanzas. Along our way to the beach house, we decide to stop at the Oasis Restaurant on A1A in St. Augustine for lunch. The sun is shining, and the temperature is ninety-three degrees. The air inside is cool, while the atmosphere is tropical Florida. Large taxidermy fish with a variety of colored scales hang along whitewashed, wooden plank walls.

The waitress comes over; I order the Mahi Mahi fish tacos. The taco is loaded with fish, sweet cabbage slaw, sharp cheddar cheese, guacamole, tomatoes, and a spicy Mexican salsa. Lizzy orders crab cakes and a Caesar salad. Mary Beth decides on boiled shrimp and a side salad with ranch dressing. Of course, everyone orders a Pina Colada. I love the skewer with fruit which they add to our drinks. Those little colorful umbrellas always make me feel like I am on vacation. Maybe I will buy some for home.

The Beach Girls are all big conversationalists. After fifteen minutes of how are the kids, grandkids, and parents, Mary Beth clues us in on a news story regarding bales of marijuana showing up on the Matanzas beach a couple of weeks ago. On a Saturday morning around seven-thirty, a couple of beachgoers walking along the beach saw something lying on the sand. As they got closer, they realized it was something that definitely didn't belong there; it was a bale of grass. They examined the bale a little closer and recognized it as marijuana. The couple immediately called the police and backed away from the bale. When the police arrived, they located ten separate bales of pot along the shore. It has a street value of over three million dollars.

Being curious and having worked for a criminal lawyer for ten years, I ask, "Do they know where it came from? Did anyone else see anything? Did the Flagler police bring in the feds?"

Mary Beth replies, "I don't know. I guess I could call Snoop Dog and see if she knows anything."

"Yes, please do that; who knows, we might find some bales on our beach at the Sea Glass House," I said.

“Yeah, wouldn't that be a party for a bunch of old girls,” Lizzy cracks up laughing. “Can you imagine Cici dancing around in circles and falling on her butt or into the ocean?” she adds.

“We couldn't carry a bale of hay, much less a bale of marijuana. Although, we could just light it on fire and have a bonfire,” I add, laughing, thinking about the girls dancing around the fire in “The Crucible.” I guess people will think we are witches.

“We'd have to drag our old, high butts back to the beach house,” adds Mary Beth.

“I would just sleep on the beach,” I say. “I would have to make sure I have enough snacks in case I get the munchies,” I add, laughing.

We all have a good laugh, especially since the three of us have never smoked a joint in our fifty-seven years. That doesn't mean I won't smoke one when they are legalized in Florida.

Our reservations wouldn't allow us to check into the Sea Glass House until four o'clock, so we decide to stop at Walgreens in St. Augustine to purchase suntan lotion and snacks. I have never worried about tanning as I have an olive skin tone which I got from my mother's side of the family. Apparently, I have Cherokee blood in my DNA. I get darker just walking out in the sun for a few minutes. Cici calls Weston and me her gingerbread couple.

Lizzy tans well and Mary Beth, bless her soul, is as white as a piece of printer paper. I purchase a fifteen SPF, Lizzy gets a thirty SPF, and Mary Beth gets a fifty SPF along with a big purple, wide-brimmed hat, white long-sleeve shirt, and a wind ninja tent to keep her from getting too much sun. I pick up some SunChips and almonds, Lizzy gets cashews and almonds, and Mary Beth picks up chocolate bars. Mary Beth has the metabolism of a hummingbird. Some of us need to take care of our skin and watch our waistlines. Luckily for us, we are all small to medium built, and I say that with a smile. We are all pretty, though; at least, our husbands thought so at one time. I'd give us an eight on the pretty scale, and when we get dolled up, we could be a nine or even a ten. Just saying.

At four o'clock, we head to the sea green-colored beach house. It is located off of old US Hghway 1 with the Atlantic Ocean no more than twenty feet from the house with its beautiful white, sandy shoreline. The house is two stories on twelve feet stilts, holding the house up from rushing waves during storms. The metal braces allow two cars to park under the house. There is room for two more cars on the sandy driveway. Twenty feet from the back of the house is a dock running into the Matanzas Inlet. Cici brought her orange, two-person canoe and placed it in the water. She ties it to the moorings on the dock and walks back toward the front of the house.

As we load our groceries and baggage up the stairs to the first floor of the house, we notice dark storm clouds on the horizon coming from the east off the Atlantic Ocean. The girls form an assembly line and move each piece of luggage, cooler, and box up the stairs. We all help each other unload the food and drinks into the kitchen and then move the luggage into the bedrooms. Once that is completed, we gather into the living space and settle in for the evening.

Lizzy and I take the king bedroom upstairs on the second floor. This floor is laid with a lush cream-colored carpet. The bedroom has a separate light blue sitting room, a bar, and a balcony overlooking the Matanzas Inlet. The luxurious, marble-tiled bathroom has a Jacuzzi tub and a walk-in shower large enough for the whole group.

Nancy and Mary Beth take one of the large bedrooms downstairs, which faces the Matanzas Inlet. Cici and Elle take the other bedroom facing the Atlantic Ocean. The first floor of the Sea Glass House consists of two bedrooms with en suites, an open floor plan living area, a kitchen, and a dining room. A powder room door faces the living area just off the entrance. A large, gray-stone fireplace (it does get rather cold in north Florida) is the focal point of the living area along with a modern, industrial metal chandelier. Above the graywood mantle sits a nautical print of high ocean waves and a schooner making its way during a storm. The grays, dark blues, and white tops of the ocean waves make the picture come alive. There are two brown leather sofas and one oversized leather armchair recliner covered with a plethora of cream and light blue pillows. A large driftwood coffee table with a glass top is arranged between the two sofas. The enormous kitchen has all the amenities, including a separate ice maker, a must for older women. One never knows when a hot flash will occur; sticking your head in the refrigerator or ice maker always helps. We are fifty-seven years old, and I have witnessed this kind of activity before. The face gets flushed, sweat dribbles down the forehead, and breathing lingers. A quick run to the freezer, head stuck in for cooling, and breathing is normal again. Ah, menopause.

After settling in, we all gather in the large, comfortable living area. It is five o'clock somewhere; time for margaritas. Cici offers to make the drinks and heads into the kitchen. "Okay, I am making margaritas," she says. "Who wants one?" Cici asks.

"I want one," I say, placing my feet on top of the coffee table and laying my head on the back cushion of the sofa. "Vacation begins," I whisper.

"Not me. I will have a sweet tea, though," says Nancy, our non-drinker. Southern girls love their sweet tea even if they move to New York. "Please add a lot of ice. I don't get much ice in my drinks at home," she adds.

Thunder roars across the dark ocean as we see bright yellow, zigzagging lightning flashing across the horizon. Five-foot waves come crashing upon the beach, and the lights of the house reflect on the water.

"It looks like this is going to last a while. I hope the lights don't go out," I say.

"Don't you worry; they have an automatic generator that will come on. I have one at the farmhouse. I made sure to ask about that when I reserved the house," says Lizzy. "You know it is not uncommon for a thunderstorm or even a hurricane during this time of year," she adds.

Our conversation gets louder by the minute as we sip our margaritas. The more relaxed we get, the funnier the conversations. The rain pours down heavily outside; small crystals of hail bounce off the living room windows. Looking out the sliding door windows, we can't see the road, ocean, or shoreline. I am glad I parked under the house. Another bolt of lightning flashes across the black sky, and thunder rolls across the open space. The lights go out, and the generator kicks in, ensuring we will have lights and air conditioning.

Nancy updates us on the new drugs being bought on the streets and the national politics in New York and Washington DC. Apparently, more and more people are dying every day with new poisonous drugs being created. Nancy tells us about her son and his wife, who have just had a new baby daughter—Nancy's first grandchild. She excitingly shows some of the first photos of her granddaughter.

Cici gives us new info in the medical field and a couple of funny stories in the ER. "Covid cases in our hospital are at a maximum. We have no ICU rooms left and I don't know what I would do if I didn't get this vacation. I have been working twelve months straight, and right now, I have to wear double masks to and from the parking lot just to get home. During the day, I wear scrubs, my bio-suit, a cloth mask, a plastic shield, and two pairs of gloves. I still don't feel safe," says Cici. "I am so tired when I get home; I don't even get to see my grandchildren," she adds.

"Dang Cici, you should just retire and get out of there!" I exclaim, frustrated. Over the last year and a half, Florida State has taken a beating with Covid. The hospitals are now using refrigerated trucks to help out the overcrowded morgues. All of us girls have gotten our vaccines except for Cici, the nurse. And wouldn't you know she is allergic to some of the chemicals in the vaccines. Her safety really worries me and the other girls.

"Anyway," says Cici, "Last week, we had a man come into the ER because he cut his wiener off."

"What?" I say with my eyes bulging out like a cartoon character.

"Well, he thought he heard the voice of God tell him that he needed to cut his penis off to save the world. It took all we could do in the emergency room to hide our shock and laughter. Thank goodness I had two masks on and double-gloved my hands. The first responders handed me the wiener!" Cici says loudly. "It wasn't very big either," she says with a snicker.

We all hoot and holler; Elle rolls onto the floor. "I guess he saved the world. We are all still here," shouts Elle.

Nancy asks, "Did y'all sew it back on?"

Mary Beth asks, "Will it still work?"

Lizzy says, "Well, that is a new one for me."

We hoot and holler some more, kicking our legs in the air and waving our arms. This continues for a couple of hours. Cici has the best stories; maybe, it is the way she tells it that makes us laugh.

Since all the Beach Girls are pretty tired, we decide to order pizza from Joe's in St. Augustine and continue our margarita blitz. The pizza arrives at eight and a bunch of hungry, old women fly to the table like a pack of wolves. Thank goodness the plates and napkins are already on the table, or we would be eating pizza like wolves. We eat our dinner of meat lovers and Hawaiian pizzas and garlic knots. After dinner, some of the girls head to their rooms to take showers and change into their pajamas. Lizzy, Mary Beth, and I finish our margaritas and clean the kitchen.

At nine o'clock, we gather again around the living area and watch the movie "Momma Mia". We sing along to the soundtrack and enjoy the fellowship with one another. When the actresses in the movie begin to sing "Dancing Queen", we raise ourselves up from the sofa and chairs and dance around the house, singing as loud as we can. In our minds, we are seventeen again and having a great time. Around noon, Nancy and Mary Beth call it a night, and the rest of us soon follow.

"Good night, Sara, Lizzy, Elle, Cici, Nancy," says Mary Beth.

"Good night, everyone," yells Nancy.

"Good night, John boy," I reply. I get a few giggles from the girls.

Chapter Nine

The next morning, I get out of bed early, around six, and go downstairs for coffee. Cici is already up, and the coffee is brewing. The aroma of fresh roast coffee, which is just ground in the grinder, is wonderful. "Good morning, sunshine," says Cici in that sweet, southern voice.

"Good morning," I moan. "What are you doing up so early?"

"I'm going to take the canoe out on the water. You want to come along?" she asks.

I reply, "Too early for me. I think I will get my coffee and sit on the balcony upstairs. Do you have your cell phone with you?" I ask.

"Yes, I stuck it here in my swimsuit top," Cici responds, pulling her phone from her bikini top.

"Good job. Be careful and wear your life jacket," I say.

"It's going to be a beautiful day on the Matanzas. I bet I will see some sea turtles. I have life jackets in the canoe; I will be careful," she responds.

I pour my coffee from the brewing pot and head back upstairs to the covered balcony. Cici was right; the view of the Matanzas Inlet was gorgeous. The sun is sparkling on the crystal, bluish-green water, which looks just like sea glass. As I sip my coffee, lounging on the tan, wicker lounger, a seagull swoops down into the inlet waters and brings up a small white fish. As the bird gently flies southward, I have the feeling that all is right in the world. Little did I know that my peacefulness was going to suddenly end.

After about fifteen minutes, Cici comes walking down the wooden, gray dock heading to her bright orange canoe. She is wearing a light green bikini with a red baseball cap tied with a thin ribbon under her chin. The baseball cap has a big, yellow sunflower on top of it and looks like a potted plant sitting on her head. I could see the top of her silver cell phone peeping from the top of her green swimsuit. What a sight is our nature girl. Her white curly hair hangs from the back of her cap. Cici picks up her blue oars and steps into the small boat as it rocks along in the water. The canoe starts to pull away from the wooden dock. She tries to balance herself by placing her arms out to her sides, but it doesn't work. She falls headfirst, red cap and all into the bluish-green water with her legs flaying in the air. She looks like a green frog stretching out, trying to catch a fly. Her head immediately pops up out of the water. I laugh so hard; I nearly fall out of the wicker lounger.

Suddenly, Cici stops and appears to be looking under the old, gray wooden dock. I slip my cell phone into the pocket of my tattered, blue jean shorts and run down the stairs heading to the dock. Cici was still staring under the dock when I ask, "Cici, what's wrong?"

Cici keeps her focus under the dock and starts to drag something from under the dock. Seaweed is hanging on the thing as she drags it into the orange canoe. She places her fingers on what appears to be the neck of a body and begins to check for a pulse. "What is it?" I asked, seeing tears gently flowing down Cici's face.

"He's dead," she whimpers.

"What are you talking about? Who's dead?" I ask.

"I just came down for my canoe ride, and as I stepped into the canoe, it started moving. I guess the body was pushing on it. I fell in and as I got back into the boat, I looked under the dock and there he was facing me. There was a bullet hole right between the eyes. I pulled him into the canoe, thinking I could help. Oh, Lordy! It was an automatic reaction that I have done in the emergency room hundreds of times," says Cici standing there in the canoe crying.

I pick my cell phone out of my shorts' pocket and call Lizzy. I knew her name was on the rental agreement and she would need to contact them too. "Lizzy, Cici just found a dead body down here under the dock. Call the police." I whisper into the phone. I try to coerce Cici out of the boat onto the dock, but she insists on staying with the body. She sits in the canoe, placing her hand on the deceased's hand and begins to pray over his body.

"Our father who art in heaven..." she says as we wait for the cops to arrive. I bow my head in prayer with her.

Within minutes, the other ladies come running down the dock with cell phones in their hands. They look like they had just spotted Kevin Costner and "Beth" from "Yellowstone." Needless to say, I had already started taking photos of the deceased and the crime scene.

The ladies are still dressed in their pajamas and nightgowns. Mary Beth has a purple tie-dyed nightgown, and Lizzy is wearing a pair of pink and gray shorty pajamas with furry slippers. Elle has on a silk pajama set with a robe. Elle forgot to put on shoes and tiptoes on the dock to keep the sand off of her feet.

As the girls continue to snap pictures with their cells, Cici announces, "The body is a male, probably in his forties, gunshot wound to the head, rope burns on his wrists and ankles. This is weird; his fingertips have been cut off and his teeth have been knocked out." Having worked in the ER, Cici knows about dead bodies and recovers from shock quiet easily. As soon as she started talking, I started recording her on my cell.

"Where's Nancy?" I ask.

"She heard 'dead body' and that was it for her. She stayed inside waiting for the cops to arrive," says Elle. "Nancy says she is still on vacation," she adds.

I continue taking pictures with my cell phone and notice a small, gold pinkie ring on the deceased's left hand, little finger. I take a quick photo and hear sirens in the distance. The sound gets louder and louder. All of a sudden, there is a mad rush of female bodies running down the dock. I have never seen those ladies' legs move so fast. They look like a group of women rushing a store on Black Friday when Christmas toys and big-screen televisions go on sale. The Beach Girls are a curious bunch. However, we are not crazy enough to hang out waiting for cops.

Flagler County's finest arrive in their green and white cop cars with sirens blaring and blue lights flashing. Two thirtysomething years old, plainclothes officers step out of the patrol car and head towards the door of the Sea Glass House. Nancy opens the door and says, "The body is down at the dock behind the house. Cici and Sara are waiting with the deceased." She is short and to the point.

"Thank you, ma'am," says the lead officer and turns around to leave. The lead officer turns back and adds, "Ma'am, please stay in the house until we tell you to come out."

"Is it okay if we go out to the beach this morning?" Nancy asks as they begin to leave. Nancy may not want to get involved, but being an agent for the DEA and on vacation from the city, she meant we were going to the beach for some sunshine.

"Okay, but don't leave the vicinity," he says with a superior tone.

The two men walk down the dock toward Cici and me. I wave to them and watch as they slowly move across the gray boards on the sundried dock glancing from side to side as if, at any minute, a gun battle would ensue. A large redfish jumps out of the blue water and both men pull their guns from the holsters attached to their belts. My first impression is just a shake of the head. "Lord, help us," I say out loud, trying not to laugh.

"My name is Detective Franks and this is Detective Ryals," the lead says. Detective Franks is a six-foot-tall, overweight, Caucasian, red-faced male. Detective Ryals is a slim, five feet and approximately eight inches tall African American. Detective Ryals has a bright smile on his face as we shake hands and looks over my head toward the inlet.

"I am Sara Springs and this is Cici Downs," I say.

Ryals says nothing, letting his eyes move back and forth, viewing the scene around him. "Who found the body?" Detective Franks asks as if doing so is wasting his time.

Cici speaks up, "I discovered the body this morning."

"Ms. Downs is it?" asked Franks with a smirk on his face.

"Yes," says Cici, still sitting in the orange canoe with the dead body.

"You can get out of the boat now," says Franks.

Cici places her right foot on the dock, and I grab her hand to help her up. Both officers stand back as if they might catch something. I guess they are worried about Covid even though neither one is wearing a mask.

"Please tell us how you came to find the deceased," Franks says.

"Well, I was going to take my orange canoe out (like there was any other canoe out there). It's the one right there," she points out. "I grabbed my oars and when I stepped into the canoe, I started floundering around and fell headfirst into the cold water. I knew something had shoved the boat because I have excellent balance. I can balance on one leg. Want to see?" asks Cici.

"No, please continue," responds Franks.

"Okay, but I can do it. Well, let me think. I got back into the canoe and noticed something under the dock. It was dark under there, so I wasn't sure at first as to what I was seeing. I was naturally curious, so I bent my head down and glanced under there. What I saw was a shock to me; it was a body. I grabbed hold of the body by the arms and dragged him into the canoe. I am an ER nurse, so my first reaction was to get him out of the water and try to help. Of course, there was nothing I could do. Sara saw me from the balcony on the first floor up there and came running down the dock," states Cici.

"I was drinking coffee on the balcony outside that bedroom," I join the conversation, pointing to the upstairs balcony.

"Sara had the cell phone and called Lizzy," says Cici.

"I called her since her name is on the rental lease. I asked her to call the police and the real estate agent," I added.

Franks asked, "Did either of you touch the body?"

"No, I didn't touch anything," I quickly say, taking a step back away from the officers.

"Didn't you listen to what I said? I told you I dragged the man out of the water and tried to help him. I took his pulse! I touched him!" yells Cici. "The deceased has a 9mm gunshot wound to the head, scrapes on his wrists and ankles and," she was quickly cut off.

Detective Franks raises his voice, saying, "Ma'am, we have an evidence team on the way and it will be here shortly. Please, just let the professionals do their jobs." Officer Ryals continues looking around the dock, avoiding Franks.

I grab Cici by the arm and walk her back down the long dock into the house. I speak up loud enough so that Franks can hear me, "Come on, Cici, let's leave the professionals to do their jobs."

The girls see us heading toward the Sea Glass House and come reeling up from the shoreline with towels and beach chairs in hand. "How did it go?" asks Lizzy.

"The tall detective was a jerk," I replied. "Other than being ignored, nothing much happened. The evidence team is supposedly on their way," I say as I head up the stairs to the house.

"Cici, let's get you in the house, and I will make you a cup of hot tea," says Nancy.

"I brought some green tea," says Elle. "It will be better for her," she adds.

"Be sure to add some of the honey I brought from home. It is better for me since it comes from the beehives near my house and helps me with my allergies," says Cici.

About thirty minutes later, the crime scene investigators arrive. Looking out of the windows, the Beach Girls watch and take more pictures with their phones. Two men in white jumpsuits walk down to the dock and another in diving gear walks behind the other men. Once at the scene, the diver goes into the water and, after a few minutes, holds up a shredded end of a rope. It looks like the rope was attached to the dead man's foot. Snap, snap, snap went our cameras. Nothing gets by the Beach Girls.

"Did you see that?" asks Elle looking out of the window with binoculars.

"What?" asks Lizzy.

"The guy that came out of the water was holding a rope which was tattered on the end," says Elle.

"Cici, did you see a rope attached to the dead man?" I ask.

"Yes, it was wrapped around his waist, but I didn't get a good look at it. I was concentrating on saving his life," says Cici sipping her green tea.

"What are they doing now?" asks Lizzy as she pushes between Mary Beth and Elle.

"They are loading the dead body onto a metal stretcher and bringing it down the dock," I say. "Close the blinds," I whisper.

Lizzy goes to the front door and sees a black hearse waiting for the body. "The hearse is out front and the men in white suits are loading the body into the back of it," she says. The two men close the door to the hearse, join the diver inside the hearse and drive away. We can hear the hearse rattle down the road back to town.

"I guess they will do an autopsy," says Cici.

After another hour or so, Detective Franks knocks on the Sea Glass front door. Talk about scrambling; cell phones are tucked under cushions, under open books, and Elle, in the kitchen, throws her cell in the dishwasher. Nancy calmly answers the door.

"Yes," she says, looking Franks in the eyes.

"Ma'am, can I have a look around in the house?" asks Franks in a pushy manner.

Nancy calmly asks, "Why do you need to look inside this house?"

"We just want to have a look around," says Franks with a disgusted look on his face.

Nancy works for the DEA in New York and I worked for fourteen years in my ex-husband's criminal law firm. We both simultaneously say, "Get a search warrant." Detective Franks has a shocked look on his face, like someone had just slapped him. The Lord knows I wanted to slap that arrogant man.

I tell Detective Franks, "We did our civic duty by calling the police after we found the body out on the dock and reported what happened to you guys. We have nothing further to do with this. You are not going to search the house, go through our luggage, or anything else. We are on vacation for four days and don't want to be bothered again with this mess. You and your professionals can look around outside all you want. Go through the trash if you want." The detective doesn't know that one of our ladies smokes marijuana for migraines, and we don't know if she brought a joint into the beach house. No one was searching this house.

Lizzy looks at the detective and says, "Detective Franks, here is the name and number of the real estate agent I have been dealing with. You can deal with her about the house. We will be leaving Monday morning, and perhaps she will give you access then."

"Thank you," says Franks. "We will be in touch if we need more information." The detective goes to his police car, slams his door, and drives away with Detective Ryals.

"Whew, Elle, did you bring your pot with you this time?" I quickly ask.

"No, I haven't had a migraine in a couple of weeks. You guys did great, but we were okay even if he searched the house," replied Elle. "I have a prescription for it, you know," she adds.

"That's a relief," I say. "There is something not right about that cop. I wouldn't want to give him a chance to put us behind bars," I add.

Nancy added, "That jerk wasn't going to search this house. We haven't done anything wrong. He just wanted to use his power to get in here. I know this kind of man. I work with them every day. Most cops are good men, but this one, I have to agree with Sara. Something is not right with him."

"The man has been dead for a few days, at least two days. They would have known that if they would have let me continue to talk," said Cici. "Can you believe that guy? I can tell he is on a power trip. Thanks, Nancy and Sara. You girls put a stop to him I love it."

"I'm going to call Snoop Dog and get the low down on Detective Franks. What's the other guy's name?" Mary Beth asks. Snoop Dog loves to investigate things for us and is really good at tracking people.

"Detective Ryals is his name. He sure was quiet, but he was definitely taking in the scene around the dock," I said.

"The rental lady, Mya, was shocked. I called her after I called the cops. I let her know what happened and she couldn't believe it. She said she would stop by later this afternoon or tomorrow. I told her to look for us on the beach. I am not giving up any more sunshine today. My beach chair is ready," said Lizzy.

Chapter Ten

"Let's have some breakfast. I am so hungry. Who's up for breakfast and then the beach?" asked Nancy. Everyone raises their hands. Nancy heads to the kitchen to make eggs, bacon, and toast.

Cici chimes in, "Make sure you use the Irish butter I brought. It is so healthy for you. It is made from the milk of grass-fed Irish cattle. Oh, and I brought my homemade blackberry jelly. I don't put any sugar in it. The ingredients are all-natural. I picked the blackberries myself."

Lizzy adds, "I brought the farm fresh eggs I gathered last week from my grass-fed, free-range chickens. The yolks are so rich; you can see how golden they are. And, they make the best cakes."

Nancy says, "I picked up some fresh bagels in New York right before boarding the plane. Yall will love them, especially the cinnamon ones. They are so delicious, especially if you put some cream cheese on them. I ate one on the plane.

I respond, "Well, y'all, I made the Bloody Mary mixture from freshly squeezed, ripe tomatoes and added tobasco sauce from the tabasco peppers I grew on the patio out by the pool." Mary Beth is sitting at the table laughing so hard she was crying. She knows I wouldn't drink a Bloody Mary and I sure as heck am not going to squeeze tomatoes. I grab a gallon of orange juice and a bottle of champagne and ask the girls, "Who's up for mimosas? I squeezed the oranges this morning and filled the bottle," I say, laughing and looking at the Minute Maid juice bottle.

After breakfast, we dress in our swimsuits, grab Mary Beth's ninja tent, and pick up the beach bags full of snacks and lotion. We grab our towels off the leather sofa in the living room as we go. The ladies slowly walk down a couple of steps on the sand dune and head to the beach. The Beach Girls spend the rest of the morning catching sun rays and sitting in their chairs at the edge of the water. There is something about hearing the ocean waves drifting into shore and the soft water rippling across our feet. Lizzy calls this her nature's pedicure.

Lizzy, Mary Beth, and I set our chairs next to the shore shading our faces with our large, brimmed hats, looking out at the ocean. Mary Beth is wearing her long sleeve white shirt and is lathered with sunscreen. She almost looks like a little mummy.

I ask Lizzy, "Liz, what do you think about this morning's events?"

Lizzy responds, "I am kind of concerned about it. We don't know if the killer is still around here."

"Do y'all think it has anything to do with those bales of pot that landed on the beach a couple of weeks ago?" asks Mary Beth.

"I don't know. It could; I wouldn't be surprised. I know that pinky ring on the dead man looked awfully familiar; I just can't remember where I have seen one of those before," I add my observation.

Lizzy pokes me in the leg and says, "Look y'all at the Octagon House over there. There is someone in there; I saw them pass by the front window."

The Octagon House is located about thirty yards from the Sea Glass House. The house is in shambles; it is obvious that no one has been there in a long while. The house is octagon in shape and made out of wood grayed by the sun. It sits on stilts off the ground with enough room underneath to park a couple of cars. The paved road ends right in front of the Sea Glass House. The only way to the Octagon House is through a chain stretched across the sand road. The chain has been locked with a stainless steel master lock. The surrounding of the house is nothing more than sand dunes that were washed ashore during the last hurricane. There is no grass or seaweed around, only driftwood and garbage which has blown under the house.

"Where's the dark truck I saw out there by the chain this morning?" I ask.

"I saw lights on at the Octagon House overnight when I got up around two this morning to go to the bathroom in the living area," Mary Beth says. "I didn't notice any truck, "she adds.

"That is strange," I say. "Could you tell what the man looked like?" I ask Lizzy.

Lizzy responds, "It was definitely a man because I saw his beard. Other than that, I haven't a clue."

"Don't say anything yet to the other girls. We will just keep a watch on the house today and tonight and see what happens," I said, getting up from my chair and heading to the tent. "I'm getting hungry," I add.

A few minutes past twelve, the rental lady, Mya, a tall blond with blue eyes and tanned skin, drives up and sees us down on the beach, soaking up the rays and water. Mya waves and comes down the steps toward our tent and chairs. "Hello, ladies; I am so sorry you had to find the deceased. I am sure we can give your money back if you would like to leave today," she says with a sweet smile.

"No!" we yell and stand up facing Mya.

"Look, we have been waiting for this vacation for a year and we are not going home because we found a dead person," says Lizzy. "Now, you can give us some of our money back for the inconvenience and the disruption of our beach time," she adds, smiling.

"Yes, that would be the prudent thing to do," I say, sliding my aviator sunglasses down on the tip of my nose.

"We can take care of ourselves and if anything else happens, we will either call you or the police," says Nancy. "I flew down here from New York and I am not ready to fly back. My tickets are nonrefundable and would cost me a lot of money," adds Nancy with a pleading look.

"Okay, ladies, look out for anything strange and stay safe. I will talk to the owners and see if we can give you back a portion of the rent," says Mya and heads back to her car.

At lunch, we all head back to the beach house for some food. Nancy pulls out a beautiful tray of fresh fruits: watermelon slices, pineapple chunks, blueberries, blackberries, strawberries, and star fruit. It looks delicious and healthy. Cici brings her homemade pimento cheese with her homemade mayo and cheese from Ireland. Lizzy makes frozen strawberry daiquiris, and Elle plays some Bob Marley music. We all dance around the kitchen, sipping our daiquiris as we sway back and forth to the reggae sounds. That's how the Beach Girls roll.

Conversation at the dining table reverts to the morning adventure. I say as I have often expressed, "We are on another adventure, girls! This could be very interesting."

Elle starts the conversation by asking, "Hey, what do y'all think is going on around here?"

Cici says, "All I can say is that the man was murdered. First, there was a gunshot wound in his head. I think it is most likely a 9mm due to the size of the hole. His fingertips were cut off and his teeth were knocked out. I didn't notice any of that when I pulled him out. I guess I was focused on trying to help him."

"Are you talking about a hit job?" I ask. "I don't think it is natural to cut off someone's fingerprints and knock their out teeth," I add with a questioning look on my face.

Mary Beth says, "I will call Snoop Dog right now and get her checking things out."

"No, not yet," I say. "Let's wait until we have more questions." I look and see that everyone has their cell phone lying on the table. "Did everybody take pictures this morning when you were down at the dock," I ask, knowing fully well they did.

Nancy immediately chimes in, "I did not take any pictures and don't want anything to do with this mess. I can't afford to get involved because of my job."

"Alright," Lizzy says. "If you want in on investigating this case, raise your hands."

Everyone but Nancy raises their hands. Nancy walks out of the dining room into the living area, where she quickly picks up her book, sits on one of the sofas, and begins reading. The others crowd around the dining room table to share their thoughts. This is not our first investigation, just our first murder. We have solved a few thefts and located, with Snoop Dog's help, a couple of lost kids.

Chapter Eleven

"Okay, everybody, please text your pictures to me. I will make copies for our investigative file. I want all of you to write down everything you saw and heard from last night through this morning, including you, Nancy!" I yell into the living room. "I will type all of the responses, too, and place them in our file," I say. I don't want to put anything on my computer as you never know who will hack it and see the information. Paper only for our file, please," I add.

Mary Beth replies, "I will get information on the detectives from Snoop Dog and write it up for the file. I will bring it to you next week when I get it typed."

Lizzy gives me a nod. I know she will follow through with the Octagon House and our mystery man. Elle stands up from the dining table with a strange look on her face as if something tastes bad. "What's the matter, Elle? Did you eat a bug?" I ask.

"Well, while y'all were talking and snapping pictures down at the dock, I grabbed a couple of strands of dark hair off our dead guy." Elle giggles and pulls out a clear, zip-lock sandwich bag with two black hairs inside. "I will buy one of those DNA kits and send it off. Don't worry, I will make up an identity and have the results sent to my post office box in the mail," she says.

"You sly, foxy lady," I say and give Elle a "high five." The other girls follow.

"Cici, will you write up any medical information you observed and anything you can add about the location of the body under the dock?" I ask. "Do you think you could get us a picture of a 9mm gunshot wound?" I add.

"Sure, I have a notebook with me and I will write everything in it and give it to you before the group heads home on Monday," says Cici. "The gunshot wound might take a while, but I know someone who works at the morgue," she adds.

"Great, ladies, I think our investigation has begun," I say. Feeling like we have covered all of our bases, I add, "Ladies, we all have some work to do when we get home, but right now, I need some sunshine and blue skies. What do y'all say?"

We head back out to the beach and enjoy the rest of the day. Having gotten enough sun for the day, Elle, Mary Beth, Nancy, and Cici head to their bedrooms to read or sleep. Lizzy and I stay outdoors on the beach to watch the dolphins and let the water and sand massage our feet. Oh, that feels so soothing. With a view like the Atlantic Ocean, who could want more? The sun is shining on the water, making little whirling motions that makes the water look like floating crystals on a blue-green satin sheet. While enjoying our afternoon, we also keep an eye on the Octagon House. I have a feeling something is not right with that place; it's that little voice inside my head.

Chapter Twelve

That evening, we order sandwiches from Ralph's, Marineland's best sandwich joint. Mary Beth and I brought a few bottles of Moscato wine. We pull them from the refrigerator right after the driver arrives with the sandwiches. Elle puts on some Michael Blublee music as we settle in for the night. We decide to watch "Yellowstone" for the third time. We all swoon as Kevin comes down the stairs into his log cabin dining room on the show wearing cowboy boots, blue jeans, and a denim shirt. We all love his character, John Dutton, as he rides and ropes just like all the macho cowboys. He is also very rich and has a beautiful ranch in Wyoming. Beth, his stage daughter, sits beside him, holds nothing back, and discusses their business deal with the bad guys. She is one badass woman; who wouldn't want to be her for a day or a week? Just saying.

Around eleven o'clock at night, we hear a loud noise outside the house coming from underneath the first floor. It sounds like someone is knocking over a garbage can. I jump up from my chair, Mary Beth grabs a pistol out of her leather purse, and other ladies head to the windows hiding behind the beige blinds with their cell phones ready. I look at Mary Beth and ask, "What are you doing with a gun?"

"I have a permit for it," she says, smiling.

"Have you ever fired that gun?" I ask, staring into her blue eyes.

"Yes, when I got my permit." Mary Beth answers.

"Get behind me and hide that gun," I whisper. Being the brave soul that I am, I slowly walk to the front door, turn on the porch light and slowly open the door. There standing next to a large, green truck, is a tall man and a slender, blond-haired woman walking under the stilts of the first floor of the Sea Glass House.

"Hey, what are y'all doing under there?' I yell. I notice a green pickup truck parked with its truck bed backed into our driveway. I can tell the woman is spooked as she stops suddenly and appears to be shaking. She is wearing blue jeans, dirty cross trainers, and a white tee shirt emblazoned with a Southern Girls logo.

The man was also wearing blue jeans and a tee shirt with a NASCAR logo. He replies, "Just picking up the garbage, ma'am"

"At eleven," I shout.

"Yes, my wife and I work days and Mya lets us pick up the rental garbage at night. I am so sorry we scared you. I guess Mya forgot to tell you," the man replies.

"She did forget. We just thought it was weird; that's all," I reply.

Mary Beth and I stay on the porch while the couple gather the black garbage cans and drop off two more. When we return to the house, I let Lizzy know what was going on so she could call Mya in the morning.

"This is just getting weirder," says Elle. "Just in case, I took a picture of the truck's tag," she adds.

"I think I got a photo of the man and woman if the picture is not too dark," says Lizzy.

"Hey, I am still drinking wine in here," slurs Cici. "I have had a no good, very sad day," she says, quoting almost verbatim from a children's story.

We finally went to bed around midnight. I notice Lizzy at the bedroom window looking out of the beige blinds toward the Octagon House. "What's going on over there?" I ask. "Is he back at the house?"

Lizzy, already dressed in her leopard pajamas and looking like a cat hiding behind a bush ready to attack, looks back from the window, wiggles her finger for me to come to the window, and says, "There is someone inside that house, look at the back window of the kitchen facing the inlet."

I look over, shocked at what I am seeing. Staring out into the night through a dirty, glass pane in the kitchen door is a bearded man. "What do you think he is doing over there?" I ask with a worried look on my face.

"It looks like he is waiting for something or someone. I have been watching him going from one window to the next. What's that sound?" she asks, turning to look at me with a frightened look on her face.

We head to the window on the front of the house and peer out of the glass. Our lights are turned off so that we can see outside. We don't see any auto lights coming from down the road. We hear a motor before seeing a truck pull up to the chain laid across the sandy, dirt road. The truck lights came on just as it approached the chain. A dark-colored, extended cab truck stops at the chain and the bearded man, dressed in black clothing and carrying a dark-colored backpack, runs from the Octagon House. I pull my phone out and rip off a couple of pictures. "Got you," I say aloud. I wonder if this man could be connected to our dead guy. "I got pictures of the bearded man, but I couldn't see the driver of the truck. It is too dark and there is very little moonlight tonight," I say. I caught him just as he came into focus in front of the headlights.

Lizzy and I get into our beds and pull the soft comforters over our shoulders. The central air conditioning in the house is kept at seventy-one degrees and is very comfortable. We discuss what we have seen for the next few minutes, then drift off to sleep. I guess all the drinking and sun have finally gotten to us. I hear Lizzy making little snoring noises as soon as she closes her eyes. When I finally go to sleep, I dream of dead bodies floating in the inlet.

The next morning, rising early again, I walk down the stairs to the quiet kitchen for my coffee. The sun is already shining brightly in the morning sky. Cici and Nancy are already up making coffee and eating breakfast at the dining table. Nancy was eating a bagel with cream cheese and Cici was munching on granola and fruit. "I made my own granola; you want to try some?" Cici asks.

Nancy, always cheerful, says, "Good morning, sweetie. You want some coffee,"

"Yes, please. Black coffee would be wonderful. No thanks on the granola," I answer, taking the cup of coffee from Nancy's hand and setting it on the countertop.

"Did you see that truck pull up last night and pick up someone from next door?" asks Cici.

"Yes, Lizzy was watching the Octagon House through the blinds and motioned me to the window," I answer. "We both saw a man get into the truck. I couldn't tell who was driving. Could you?" I ask.

"No, it was pretty dark out there. I think it was a waning moon," says Cici. "You know you can't see anything when there is a waning moon," she adds, placing a spoonful of her granola into her mouth.

Nancy hands me my cup of coffee in an insulated cup and walks out on the porch with her coffee and bagel smothered with cream cheese, trying her best to avoid the dead man and the murder investigation.

"I have a feeling that the Octagon man has something to do with our murder victim," I say to Cici.

"I agree. The timing is too close for it not to be connected," says Cici. Cici heads for the porch and asks Nancy, "Hey Nancy, you want to go on a canoe ride in the Matanzas?"

"Yeah, I'll go," said Nancy. "Let me get my swimsuit on and pick up my hat. You do have life vests, right?"

"Ye yas, I have two life jackets in the boat. You can swim, the shoreline is within thirty yards each way," says Cici sarcastically. "Besides, you know I am a great swimmer and a great boater," she adds, rolling her eyes.

"Yes, I know you are the best swimmer ever," laughs Nancy as she heads into their bedroom to get dressed.

I laugh at the two ladies and head up to the bedroom balcony on the second floor. The sun reflecting on the blue-green water looks like shimmering diamonds; it is a beautiful morning. Two white seagulls dive into the crystal water, gather their breakfast, and fly to the shore before dropping the fish onto the beach. Cici and Nancy soon come down the dock laughing. Cici has a bright orange bikini and a red cap with a flower. Nancy has a blue and white striped, one-piece, low-cut swimsuit with her Yankees baseball cap. I yell, "Don't bring back any more dead bodies, and stay out of trouble!"

Cici laughs, and Nancy waves me off with her hand.

"Maybe I will see some sea turtles today or some good-looking live man!" yells Cici.

Lizzy arrives with a cup of coffee with almond milk and a couple of teaspoons of honey. "Mmm," she says, tasting her coffee. She joins me on the bedroom balcony and takes a seat on a wicker chair. "I have an idea," she says, looking down at me with her sunglasses sliding down the top of her nose.

"What?" I ask, looking up at her with my eyes closed due to the sun's glare.

"How do you feel about going diving today?" Lizzy asks with a grin on her face.

"I don't know how to dive; I could snorkel, though. We are talking about checking out the inlet for clues, aren't we?" I question with a smile on my face.

"Yes, I was thinking we could borrow Cici's canoe this afternoon when the girls are down at the beach or napping. We can drive over to Salty's Dive Shop in St. Augustine this morning and rent some equipment." Lizzy responds.

"Sounds good to me," I say.

We dress in jean shorts and pink tees which say "Beach Girls' Weekend" on the front, grab our shoulder purses, and go out to the SUV.

Lizzy drives the SUV since she knows how to get to Salty's. We head down A1A enjoying the views of the blue ocean and white beaches. It takes only twenty-five minutes to get to the dive shop. The outside of the shop is painted coral with a blue ocean mural. The artist painted a diver in the water with full gear and placed a variety of colorful fish and a dolphin swimming around the diver. The owner, Jimmy, opens the door and waves us inside; he recognizes Lizzy. "Hey, Lizzy girl, did you ever get enough weights to keep your butt from floating up?" he asks, laughing.

"Hey, Jimmy. You still remember that?" she asks. "I didn't think I could float like that being so small. It was funny trying to dive and my body floating back up to the surface," she adds.

"Are you kidding? We must have placed three weights in that belt on you before you stopped floating. We usually use those kinds of weights for men. You are a buoy, girl. What can I do for you pretty ladies today?" he asks, giving me a wink.

"This is my friend, Sara, and we would like to rent some diving equipment," states Lizzy.

"I don't dive, so I will just need snorkeling gear," I say, giving him a smile and a wink.

"Lizzy, do you still have your diving certificate?" asks Jimmy as he heads over to the snorkeling equipment.

"Yes, I was just down in Key Largo a month ago and went diving down in the Keys. Have you ever heard of Reef Divers Shop?" Lizzy asks Jimmy.

"Yeah, my friend Mikey owns the place. Did he take you out in his boat?" asks Jimmy.

"Yes. The coral reefs were beautiful, although there seemed to be fewer every time I dive in the Keys, but the fish were everywhere. I saw a hammerhead shark and a barracuda," replies Lizzy.

"It is beautiful in the Keys," says Jimmy. "You can still see some amazing things snorkeling in the Atlantic Ocean," he adds, looking my way.

I head over to the snorkeling gear and try on some flippers to make sure they fit my small feet, size six.

"That's okay; I have all the equipment you will need. Are you girls going any place special?" Jimmy asks.

"No, just thought we would look around the inlet for a little bit this afternoon. It is such a beautiful day, and the water looks amazing. We are hoping to see some colorful fish or sea turtles or maybe, both," replies Lizzy.

Jimmy gathers up our equipment, loads it into the SUV, and Lizzy hands him her credit card. He rings the equipment up as Lizzy slips her credit card into the machine. She punches a few buttons, and off we go. "Thanks, Jimmy!" we both yell as we drive off toward the Sea Glass House.

Once we arrive back at the Sea Glass House and store our equipment under the house in the small, wooden tool shed connected to one of the stilts, we head upstairs to get into our swimsuits. The other girls are out at the beach; we decide to join them. They had put up the blue wind ninja tent. We place our beach chairs near the water; it is time for some feet cooling, beach rays, and the amazing sound of God's ocean waves. We are in paradise once more.

Around one o'clock, we decide to go up to the Sea Glass House for lunch. Today, Mary Beth, Lizzy, and I are making lunch. Lizzy and I head upstairs to shower first and get dressed for lunch. Nobody likes a sandy swimsuit or sand everywhere on their body when they are eating. I shower first, put on my jean shorts and coral tee, and head down to prepare lunch.

I pull out the gas grill and light it up; salmon on the grill for today's lunch. I marinade the bass with teriyaki sauce mixed with a bit of brown sugar and let it rest in the refrigerator for thirty minutes. Mary Beth is making yellow rice with sweet peppers, and Lizzy is making her special salad; mixed greens, walnuts, strawberries, blueberries, and Colby Jack cheese. She uses raspberry vinaigrette to lightly toss with the other ingredients. Elle opens some white wine she purchased from a winery in Orlando. I pick up the wine glass, swirl the wine in my glass, and take a sip. I make a little mew sound like a cat as the taste is delicious; my mouth wants more.

We fill our plates and sit at the dining room table for lunch. The others taste the salmon, rice, and salad. "Yummy," says Cici. "This food is great. I love the salmon. Yall made a great, nutritional meal. You know I only use sea salt on my fish."

"I used sea salt on the salmon, Cici," I say.

Elle adds, "This salad is delicious; what did you put in it?"

Lizzy responds, "Everything but tomatoes. I don't like tomatoes, but if you want some, I cut one up and it is on the kitchen island. I'll bring it to the table."

Lizzy goes over to the island and brings the tomatoes. "I'd like a few tomatoes," I say. "Just sprinkle a few pieces onto my salad," I add, holding my salad plate.

"Mary Beth, I like the rice. I thought the peppers would be hot, but they are just sweet and crunchy," says Nancy.

"Yall know I don't like anything hot. I bought some of those small, orange, and yellow sweet peppers and put them in with the rice. I did remove all the seeds from the peppers." states Mary Beth.

"Elle, I love that keto cookie you made with the almond flour. What is in it?" I ask.

"It is a Honey Chocolate Crunchy cookie," says Elle. "I use almond flour, coconut oil, and one egg. I put a quarter cup of honey in it. I also added vanilla flavoring to give it a better taste and a pinch of salt."

"Text me the recipe, please. I really like it. I think I can add some ginger to the recipe for the holidays," I respond.

"That sounds like a good idea. I might try that too," says Elle.

Once lunch is over, Lizzy and I grab Cici and ask, "Can we borrow your canoe for a little while? We want to go out in the Matanzas inlet for a little bit."

"Sure, y'all have fun. The life jackets are in the canoe under the seats. I am going to take a nap and then go down to the beach later," she answers. "I need a little beauty sleep to rest my brain," Cici adds.

Our next move is to involve Mary Beth in our mission. Mary Beth is alone in the kitchen, cleaning up the table. "Mary Beth," I whisper. "This morning, Lizzy and I rented some diving equipment. We are going out in the canoe to look for clues. We need you to make sure no one comes around Matanza's side. Most of the ladies are taking a nap or going down to the beach. We should only be gone for no more than an hour. Do you think you can handle them till then?"

"Sure, I can keep a watch for y'all," says Mary Beth. She looks at me, "You can't dive. Yall, please be careful, and if you find anything, you better tell me."

"Okay," I say and head out the door with Lizzy. "I'm snorkeling," I say.

After walking down the stairs, we get our equipment out of the shed, ensure no one is looking, and hustle down the empty dock to the orange canoe. The sun is shining brightly; I have to duck my head to keep the glare off of my sunglasses. I load our equipment into the boat and throw a small, blue, plastic tarp over it. We grab the lifejackets from under the seats and put them on. We really don't need them as we both are good swimmers, but if someone is watching, we don't want to look suspicious. It is a good habit to do so. One never knows what can happen on the water.

Once in the boat, Lizzy and I grab the oars, and off we go to the broken-down dock of the last house on our peninsula; it is the pale yellow siding, single-story house. No one goes there since the road is washed out, and the roof of the house is falling into the living area. Although, as we pass the dock of the Octagon House next to the last house, I notice that the dock piers are made of cement and fairly new.

Once we get to the yellow house, I help Lizzy into her equipment and hand her the underwater camera I purchased at Salty's that morning. Lizzy sits backward on the edge of the canoe and falls into the water. She rises up out of the water and gives me a "thumbs up" sign. NEVER DIVE ALONE.

After tying up the canoe to the old dock, I put on my snorkeling gear and jump into the water. I see Lizzy underneath and watch as she swims around the edge of the dock. All of a sudden, a big, green sea turtle swims right into my left thigh. I turn quickly in that direction. It was a big momma turtle; she was staring me right in the face. She must be the size of a small, round kitchen table and looked a lot like Donatello from the

Nnja Turtles movie. I think she is as scared as I am I quickly swim one way, and she goes the other way. I head to the canoe and pop my head out, laughing and trying to gather some air. So much for my bravery; that turtle scared me.

I jump back into the blue water with my goggles to keep an eye on Lizzy. She continues to move slowly around the bottom sand beneath the dock. I see her touching something and watch as she takes pictures of whatever she is holding. I couldn't tell what it was through my goggles. Lizzy turns around and motions me to go up with a wave of her hand.

Lizzy comes out of the inlet water a few minutes later and takes off her oxygen tank and goggles, handing them to me in the canoe. She then pulls herself up and slides into the boat. "Well, what did you see?" I ask.

"Well, I saw a big turtle chasing you like a dog chases a cat! I took a couple of pictures. It was hilarious watching you flap those legs swimming in one direction and the turtle swimming in the other direction," she laughs. "There's nothing here. Let's move over to the Octagon House dock," she adds, motioning to the next house. Lizzy and I each take an oar and paddle our way to the dock.

I help Lizzy once again with her diving equipment. She slides into the blue water near the new dock. I jump in next with my snorkeling gear and swim around the outside of the dock, making sure there are no momma sea turtles around. Lizzy examines the cement piers. I see her pick up something from the sand bottom near one of the piers. She motions me to head up to the boat and follows me, carrying something in her hand.

I get into the canoe, and she hands me a piece of cement. I help her into the boat and ask, "What did you see down there?" I ask.

"I did see a brown rope tied to one of the cement piers of the dock and took some pictures. You could see where the rope was wrapped to the new dock; the sheared end of the rope was still attached. I guess that storm on Thursday night must have sheared it. It was a terrible storm; the rope must have broken loose with the body. Apparently, they couldn't find a concrete block, so they tied the rope around the cement piling," Lizzy says. "You know, I picked up a small piece of the concrete spillage which was lying around the bottom of the pier. I can have one of the concrete techs, I have used in the past, examine it for its chemical makeup."

"You can do that?" I ask.

"Sure, a lot of times, the feds check out cement chemical makeup, especially if they are looking into construction disasters. There is a company in Jacksonville that can check out the concrete. The makeup of the concrete will indicate who made that particular concrete mixture. The results also can tell when it was made and if it includes any abnormalities," says Lizzy.

"That is impressive. Okay, you take care of that. Let's not mention any of this to the others," I say. "I think we should take a look around the

Octagon House too a little before you dive again. I don't want to leave you alone diving. This house is kind of spooky."

I tie off the canoe to the weathered dock; Lizzy and I get out and walk up the long dock to the house. We notice a few footsteps in the sand around the dock and assume it belongs to the bearded man. Lizzy takes a couple of pictures of the footprints with my goggles next to them for measurement. We go up the wooden stairs to the surrounding porch and look into the grimy back window. Someone has been eating fast food in the kitchen, as there are McDonald's burger wrappers and paper cups on the kitchen table. We look in the dirty, gray windowpanes of the living area and see old newspapers on the floor.

"Look, Lizzy. There is that article Mary Beth told us about, the article about the bales of pot on the beach. Do you think this is all connected; It sure looks like it," I add.

"Yes, Sara, I think you might be right," she says, moving to the next window, which appears to be a bedroom window. Peeking between dragging blinds, we see a mattress and blanket on the floor in the center of the room

"There is an old mattress lying on the floor and an old, thin, blue blanket. I see some old food wrappers lying on the hardwood floor next to the mattress," Lizzy says.

"I think we better get out of here," I say, grabbing Lizzy's arm and escorting her around to the back of the house and speeding down the stairs toward the dock.

Before we head back to Sea Glass House, Lizzy makes one more dive around the Octagon House's dock. She finds nothing and comes back up from the water.

"I don't think we need to do any more diving or investigating today. We need to think about this for a while before drawing any conclusions. Let's get back and find out if Mary Beth has had any time to speak to Snoop Dog," I say.

We row the boat to the dock behind the Sea Glass House, tie up the orange canoe, and hide our equipment in the wooden shed underneath the first floor of the house where we had parked the cars. The other Beach Girls are still on the beach, sitting under the blue tent, each holding a glass of something. So, we head down to the beach to join them

"Hey, where have you two been?" asks Elle sitting in her multicolored, striped beach chair, stretching her long legs and drinking a glass of sweet "assed" tea.

"We took the canoe out for a little while. I saw a big momma sea turtle; she was as close as we are. She scared the crap out of me," I said, making my eyes wide.

Chapter Thirteen

"We were talking about going to the Crazy Anglers' lounge this evening," says Cici. "I think we should do some drinking and dancing. Nancy, I know you dance, and you can drink diet coke," she adds.

"That sounds great; we can boogie-woogie," I say, dancing around in my two-piece black, high-cut swimsuit with my hands waving.

"Sounds great to me!" says Lizzy as she does a little shuffle with her bare feet and wiggles her little butt.

"Let's grab some food at the bar," says Mary Beth. "After that big lunch, I don't want very much to eat," she adds.

"Okay, we will head out around seven and grab something to eat at the Crazy Anglers," I say. "Let's go up around five to get our showers, have a cocktail and get dressed," I add.

"You had me at cocktails," says Elle. "What are y'all wearing?" she asks.

"I have a pink sundress; I will wear that with my gold sandals," I answer.

"My dress is lavender with tiny white dots. It is so hot today; other clothes will be unbearable for me," says Lizzy.

"I have a 'pur-pel' flowered sun dress that I brought. I think I will wear it with my brown leather flip-flops," says Cici.

"I am wearing capris and my blue top with the cold shoulders," says Mary Beth. "I think it is sexy," she giggles.

"I am wearing capris, too," adds Nancy.

Elle, who has long legs, says, "I am wearing a short green skirt and white lace blouse."

"You and your short skirts and long legs. It must be nice to have those legs," I say. "I am so jealous. Ok, girls, we have a plan for tonight!" I yell.

By seven, we are all dressed in our sexy clothes and classy makeup. We may be fifty-seven, but we still look pretty good when we want to. We will turn a few heads tonight and, hopefully, not get into any trouble.

We decide to drive two cars; Lizzy, Mary Beth, and I get into my SUV. The others drive Elle's Trail Blazer. We pull out onto A1A and head into Palm Valley for our night on the town. The parking lot to Crazy Anglers' lounge was almost full. We find two parking places, glance at our little mirrors to check our makeup and hair, and walk indoors. This place is rocking, and we are ready to party. The wooden dance floor is almost two-thirds full, and the band sounds great. We locate a large table on the second tier and wind our way around the dance floor.

Once seated, the waiter, Jamie, arrives at our table to take our drinks order. "He is a fine specimen of the male species," whispers Mary Beth as she stares at the guy.

I order a screwdriver. "Little on the vodka," I say, wanting to keep my senses about me. Lizzy and Mary Beth order margaritas. Cici and Elle order glasses of white wine, and Nancy orders a diet Coke.

Fifteen minutes later, the drinks arrive, and Mary Beth, in a southern drawl, asks, "Jay mee, can we have some 'men yous, pleeze?'" The rest of us turn our heads to keep from laughing.

The band's first song of the night is "Sweet Caroline", which we all sing loud and proud. After all, my granddaughter's name is Caroline, and I sing that song to her all the time. I don't think she likes it very much, but then again, she never stops me from singing. Jamie returns with the menus, and we order all kinds of hors d'oeuvres: fried squash, cheese sticks, fried mushrooms, chips and salsa, boiled shrimp or, as Cici says in her southern drawl, "bald shrimp" and spring rolls. Cici also orders "sweet assed tay" with her meal. I translate her order to Jamie.

Jamie smiles, gives us a wink and takes our menus. He is making sure he gets a big tip tonight.

"Wow! That man is built. Look at those muscles," says Lizzy staring at the waiter.

"He is fine," says Mary Beth. "Just saying," she adds.

The band starts playing "Old Time Rock n Roll", and we girls step down to the brown, wooden dance floor to strut our stuff. One thing about us Beach Girls is that we can all dance. The beat starts, and the butts start wiggling. By the end of the song, we had a group of men and women dancing around with us. We had them all raising their arms in the air and wiggling their butts. What fun! The food gets served, and we sit around the table, eating, drinking, and singing along with some of our favorite songs.

"Satisfaction by the Rolling Stones," cries the DJ while the band takes a break. We all start singing along to the Stones. "I can't get no sat-is-fact-ion!"

"This is a great night!" I yell after taking another drink from my glass.

"Here's to the Beach Girls!" yells Cici lifting her glass of wine.

"Yeah!" adds Nancy dancing next to the table. By midnight Nancy had switched to ginger ale.

Nancy knows all the words to the songs and sings every single one. Jamie, the handsome waiter, joins her in singing "Under the Board Walk". The other Beach Girls love watching Nancy and Jamie sing as they gaze into each other's eyes to keep in sync.

After the song, Mary Beth jumps up and grabs Jamie to sing the next song, "You've Lost that Loving Feeling", with her. They are pretty good together as singers only. Jamie is at least twenty-five years younger than us, and Mary Beth, as lovely as she is, doesn't have a chance with the young man.

By one o'clock, we were done. Mary Beth is in a dark corner trading kisses with a good-looking man who is tall, has gray hair, and built like a basketball player. I walk over to them and say, "Mary Beth, give him your number. We are out of here."

Mary Beth giggles, tells him her number and grabs my arm. "He is really cute, isn't he? His name is Nelson, and he is from Connecticut. Nelson is a pilot for Trans-East Airlines. He and his buddies have been fishing, and he caught a big red snapper today," she says.

"The snapper is you. Come on, I am taking you home," I say, laughing and grabbing her arm, escorting her out the door. "I am glad you had a good time," I add as we shuffle to the car.

Lizzy and I let Mary Beth tell us all about her new man on the way back to the Sea Glass. Apparently, Nelson likes the way she giggles and said he likes petite women with big boobs. We arrive at the Sea Glass House with Mary Beth still giggling. I grab her by the arm and lead her inside and to the bedroom. I take her shoes off and help her get in bed. Then, I pull the coverlet over her small body. She is asleep as soon as her head hits the pillow. I guess she had a few too many drinks tonight. Good for her.

Chapter Fourteen

The next morning we get up early, except for Mary Beth, who is still sleeping. "This is our last day," I say. "What are the plans?" I ask, looking at the girls seated at the kitchen table.

The decision was made to stay out on the beach for our last day. Lizzy and I go ahead of the others and set up the wind ninja. We place our beach chairs closer to the ocean to soak our feet. As Elle walks across the sand dune, she stumbles and twists her right ankle. Beach Girls to the rescue! We all run to help her. Elle is 5 feet 10 inches tall, and we still pick her up. I grab her right foot, Lizzy grabs her left foot, Mary Beth, who has finally joined the group, grabs under her right arm, and Nancy grabs under her left arm. We carry her to a beach chair under the wind ninja. We look like laying her out for a cult sacrifice. Cici, the nurse, comes running from the Sea Glass House with a stethoscope wrapped around her neck, an emergency kit in one hand and a bag of ice in the other. After inspection, Cici tells everyone that Elle is okay, just a minor sprain and scrape on her arm where Mary Beth dropped her into the chair. She puts a band-aid over the scrape and a bag of ice on Elle's ankle.

"Elle, I will make you a cup of hot tea," says Nancy gently.

"Heck no; bring me a cold glass of wine," says Elle.

"Okay," says Nancy reluctantly.

After fearing for Elle's life, we continue our plan. Our last day is rather quiet as we contemplate reality. We feel this way every year; a little sad but happy we get to share this fellowship of friends.

At lunch, we finish up the leftovers and clean the kitchen. We decide to go out to dinner rather than messing up the kitchen again. Elle, Cici and Nancy decide to take a nap and head to their bedrooms. Lizzy, Mary Beth, and I head back to the beach.

"Mary Beth, did you get to talk to Snoop Dog?" I ask, turning to look her way.

"Yes, she called me back this morning. Apparently, Detective Franks is not well-liked at the sheriff's office. According to Snoop Dog's husband, Jason, the detective has a reputation for being lazy and has the most unsolved cases in his unit. Snoop Dog said she met Franks once and didn't like him then. She said he is arrogant and a slob," says Mary Beth.

"No doubt about that. Did you ask her about the bales of pot?" Lizzy asks.

"I did ask, and she said she would get back to me on that. The only thing she knew was that they had not located the drug dealers or how it got on the shoreline," said Mary Beth.

"Well, I guess, we will be on our own for this investigation. Looks like Detective Franks is not going to be much help," I stated.

Chapter Fifteen

At five o'clock, we decide to head up to the house to shower and get ready for dinner. After showering and dressing, we all meet up in the living area. Nancy speaks up, "Let's go to the Shrimp Hut for dinner. This is the last time I will get fresh Florida seafood for a while. After all, it is my last night," she says with her sad, puppy face.

"That sounds great. I need to drop off something at Salty's before dinner, so Sara, Mary Beth, and I will meet y'all there. Hey Nancy, what time is your flight tomorrow?" Lizzy asks.

"I have to be at JAX by twelve as the plane leaves at two. It will probably take an hour or so to check in with all the Covid protocols," Nancy replies.

"I am going to drop her off at the airport on my way home," says Cici.

Lizzy says, "Schedule check-out time is ten; if y'all want to, we can leave a little early and stop on our way home for brunch."

"That sounds like fun," says Elle.

"Works for me," Nancy replies.

"Those wedge sandals are so cute," I tell Lizzy. "They match your dress perfectly. Both have pink and yellow flowers with green leaves. The design in the material is a perfect match; how on earth did you get them to match?" I add.

"I like your sundress with those pockets; I love pockets," says Elle. "The shoes are fabulous, too," she adds.

"I have had these shoes for over ten years. I found them up in the closet. I bought the dress a couple of weeks ago from a little boutique in Amelia Island. The place is called Sassy's. When I placed the two next to each other, I couldn't believe they were a match," says Lizzy.

We head out to the Shrimp Hut for dinner. As we go walking through the dining area, I notice little pieces of white stuff on the floor. It looked like some type of styrofoam. This place is pretty crowded, so we wait at the bar for about fifteen minutes before our table is ready. A waitress comes to take us to our table, where I see more of the strange styrofoam pieces. It looks like a trail around the restaurant.

Once seated, we all order boiled shrimp and side salads. The boiled shrimp at the Shrimp Hut are always fresh, large, and delicious. The cocktail sauce has just enough spice to make your mouth tingle. In the middle of the table is a big metal bucket for depositing our shrimp shells and a couple of tea light candles set in small, clear glass globes are placed on both sides of the table. While at the table, I bring up next year's beach trip, "Hey, y'all want to come back to the Sea Glass House next year?"

I notice Lizzy acting strange and ask, "What's the matter, Lizzy?"

She lifts her feet under the table and says, "Look."

I look under the table; the right sole of her shoe has come off. That was the trail I saw on the floor of the restaurant! The white stuff was her shoe falling apart. I start laughing, and then all the other girls look under the table to see what I am laughing at. Lizzy says, "I have to go to the bathroom. Can I borrow your shoes?"

I immediately take off my gold leather sandals and slide them under the table toward Lizzy. "Sure," I say. Lizzy slides on my two-sizes-too-big-for-her-feet shoes and drags her feet to the restroom. She wears a size four wide and has a heck of a time finding shoes. She looks like a penguin shuffling across the floor. When Lizzy returns to our table, she pushes the sandals toward me. I giggle and slide my sandals back on. Good thing she is short, and her feet don't touch the floor.

We all agree to return to the Sea Glass House next year. Our food arrives and all conversation comes to a halt. The best way to get a bunch of women to stop talking is to feed them; this is no exception.

We finish our meals, pay our bills and then, Lizzy grabs her disintegrated shoes from under the table and places them in the tin bucket on the driftwood table. We all laugh, get up from the table, take off our shoes, and follow Lizzy out of the restaurant barefooted. We wave our shoes in the air like we just don't care as the other customers watch. The men at the bar clap and hoot as we head out to our cars. What a sight we are.

When we get back to Sea Glass House, we decide to play bingo for money. Every year the Beach Girls bring twenty dollars each and we place the money in a pile on the dining room table. Cici brings her Bingo game and we play three games. Elle passes out the Bingo cards and Mary Beth passes out the tokens to be placed on the cards when the numbers are called.

"The prize for the first game is twenty dollars," I say.

"What's the prize for the next two?" asks Nancy. "Can we buy in for more cards?" she adds. Lizzy and I look at each other with a grin. Now we know Nancy's vice.

"Not this year. Next year we will let everyone who wants to bring twenty dollars for a card and buy more cards at twenty dollars each," I say.

Nancy says, "Yes!" She throws her arms into the air and does her Bingo dance.

"Looks like Nancy had been visiting Bingo halls in New York," I say.

Cici calls out, "B-ee fo-or."

"B-ee fo-or," I say, laughing. Cici can make a two-syllable word out of one letter.

I win the first game, and, of course, its winnings are the lowest amount of money. Cici wins the second game, and Nancy wins the big money. We take pictures of the winners and a picture of the losers. Everyone is still happy as we all head to the kitchen for snacks. Elle has sliced and diced fresh celery sticks, cucumbers, tomatoes, a variety of sliced peppers, and tiny blocks of cheese. Mary Beth has made her special cheese dip and places it with some chips on a plate on the marble kitchen island. I pour some ranch dressing to be used with the fresh vegetables into a small bowl and place them on the island.

After Bingo and our snack time, Lizzy and Mary Beth decide to play Phase Ten. They are the queens of the card game, Phase Ten. We gather our wine glasses and the Phase Ten cards and head to the dining room table. All the Beach Girls are competitive; we each like to win. Elle wins the first round and after about two hours, I beg out of the game and head to my room to gather my things and pack my luggage.

I slowly walk upstairs to the bedroom and hear the girls laughing and yelling along the way.

"Why are you hitting my hand," yells Elle.

"I've told you five times that you have to pick up a card before you lay down cards," laughs Mary Beth. I hear a sound that is like a pop.

"My momma has never hit me!" yells Elle laughing.

"Well, she should have," replies Mary Beth. I could hear all the ladies laughing and having a good time.

After sitting down in a chair on the balcony, I give Weston a call. He answers on the third ring. "Hey, baby, what you doing?" I ask.

"I just made myself a sandwich. Are you and the girls having a good time?" he asks.

"Yes, we have had a great time. I should be home by lunchtime tomorrow. We are stopping on the way home to have brunch before Nancy has to go to the airport," I reply.

"Okay, be careful, and I will see you when you get home. Miss you and love you," says Weston.

"I love you, too," I say and hang up the phone.

I hear sounds coming from downstairs and lean over the stair railing, "Hey, ladies! Weston said to tell everyone hello," I yell.

I laugh and go into the closet to remove my clothes from the hangers in the large walk-in closet. I place them into the luggage I have opened on the bed. I always bring too many clothes and shoes; trying to stuff them back into the suitcase is a struggle.

At twelve, Lizzy comes up the stairs and sees me glancing out at the Octagon House. I could hardly see it, but there was a small light moving around in the kitchen area near the backdoor. Lizzy moves in close behind me, pushing one of the blinds up so she can see and asks, "What do you see?"

"I think someone is in the house. Look at the kitchen window," I say, moving my head closer to the window blinds.

"I see a small beam of light moving around inside the kitchen like the orb of a ghost. It looks like light from a flashlight or some spooky ghost orb. I can't tell if there is a person holding the light. It is too dark," Lizzy says.

"Do you see a truck by the chain on the road?" I ask, watching Lizzy move toward the front window.

"No, it is so dark; it is hard to see that far. I can't even see the ocean down there," says Lizzy.

We continue to watch as the beam of light moves from room to room in the Octagon House. It is so dark outside that we couldn't see a face. We assume the bearded man must have returned, but we are so tired from all the sun today that our eyes can barely stay open. We stay by the window for a few more minutes, but nothing happens. The light disappears, and the house is completely dark.

"I am going to bed," I say, going into the bathroom to change into my nightgown.

"Goodnight, Sara. I am right behind you," Lizzy whispers.

The next morning we rise early, around seven, and meet the other Beach Girls downstairs in the kitchen. Elle is making another pot of hot coffee; the others are cleaning the refrigerator, freezer, and pantry. Each girl has a cooler for their refrigerator items and a large box for their dry goods.

I look around at all the ladies placing their items into the containers and say, "I guess this means we are going home."

"Yeah, it looks like another beach trip is ending," says Lizzy sadly.

With luggage, food and beach chairs loaded, we gather into the autos and head towards Jacksonville. Lizzy stops by Salty's Dive Shop to drop off the scuba and snorkeling gear. "Come back soon," says Jimmy as we exit his shop.

We stop at Cracker Barrel since we all love their southern comfort food and gift items. After brunch and a little shopping, we all hug one another. I yell, "Love y'all," as we get into our cars. Back to reality: jobs and families.

Chapter Sixteen

A few weeks later, Mary Beth and Lizzy bring their grandkids over to swim with Caroline, my granddaughter, who is nine years old. Mary Beth's daughter is going on a birthday trip with her husband, Jason, so Mary Beth is keeping twelve years old Jackson. He looks just like Opie on the television series, 'The Andy Griffith Show'. Rhilyn, Lizzy's ten years old granddaughter, wanted to spend time on the farm since her brother, Bryson, was going with her mom and dad to play in a golf tournament in Orlando. Rhilyn loves to swim and visit her Aunt Sara.

"Aunt Sara, watch me dive!" yells Rhilyn. She straightens her arms, stands on tiptoes, and makes a beautiful dive into the deep end of the swimming pool. Her dark brown hair flows across her back as she swims.

"Great dive, Rhilyn," I say, smiling and clapping.

Lizzy jumps out of her chair, claps her hands and yells, "Rhilyn, that was amazing!"

"Nana, watch me slide onto the float!" yells Caroline.

She climbs up the ladder, sits down, and using her hands, pushes her little butt behind down the slide. She lands full out on the aqua float without making a splash. Her long legs arrive first on the float, and then her body follows in a sitting-up position.

"Great job Caroline. That's a ten!" I yell. Caroline has a big teethed smile on her pretty little face.

"Watch Jackson," says Mary Beth. Jackson puts on his little blue goggles and jumps into the pool. He swims underwater the entire length of the pool, which is about thirty feet. He pops his head out of the water and looks at us sitting at the table.

"Wow, Jackson, you swim like a fish," I say. We all clap for the grandkids.

Kids are great. I love it when they show off in front of other children. My cell phone, which is sitting on the table, rings. "Hello."

Nancy replies, "Hi, Sara. How are you? I didn't catch you at a bad time, did I?"

"No. Mary Beth, Lizzy, and the grandkids are here swimming. Hold on a second; I am going to put you on the speakerphone," I say. "What's up?" I ask.

"Hey, everybody," says Nancy. "I was wondering if you could send me the picture of the bearded man from the Octagon House. I saw a quick glimpse of it when you took my picture at the beach, and you let me see it on your cell. Last week, I was looking at some pictures in the office, and I think one of them could be him," Nancy says.

Lizzy chimes in, "I am sending the picture to you now."

"What are you thinking, Nancy?" Mary Beth asks.

"I am not sure, and I don't want to get your hopes up. Let me check it out, and if something comes up, I will let you know," replies Nancy.

"Stay in touch, girl. Love you," I say. I look at the other ladies and shrug my shoulders.

My husband, Weston, is over at the gas grill cooking hot dogs and yells, "Hotdogs are ready, gang! Come and fix your plates."

Nancy says, "Ok, girls, I will let you go. Have a great day with the grandkids."

"Miss you," I say and hang up the phone. "That was an interesting call."

"Yeah, I guess she is thinking about the case," says Mary Beth.

"I knew she was interested, but due to her job at the DEA, she did not want to get involved," I say.

"I can't blame her," says Lizzy going over to the grill to make a plate for Rhilyn.

We prepare the kids their hot dogs and enjoy the rest of the afternoon, watching them swim and dive.

Chapter Seventeen

Halloween is around the corner; I decorate the house with pumpkins, spiders, and skeletons. I even hang little white cloth ghosts in the trees. Each year we have around a hundred ghosts and goblins stop by the house for a treat or even a trick once in a while. This year Weston dresses like a werewolf and hides behind the big oak tree in the front yard. The first three children are under six, so Weston stays hidden behind the tree. The kids are dressed as Superman, Wonder Woman, and a tiny ghost. The ghost is only a year old, and Wonder Woman, who is six years old, is pushing the ghost in a stroller. These are my neighbor's kids, and they look adorable.

"Trick or Treat!" they cry.

I open the door and exclaim, "Wow, look who is visiting me! Do I know you?" I ask.

A tiny voice speaks out, "Mrs. Springs, I am Lila from next door. This is my Wonder Woman costume."

"Well, my goodness. You are Lila. Who is this?" I ask, pointing to Superman.

"I'm Rickey," says Lila's brother Rickey.

"Then, this must be little Tommy," I say.

"Treat," says Tommy the Ghost.

The next group consists of our grandchildren. Caroline is dressed as a mermaid, shimmering tail and all. Rylan is wearing a business suit and looks like the President of the United States with a tie and a flag tie tack. His hair is slicked back and has aviator sunglasses on. Brooks is a football player zombie with blood oozing down his face and a ripped-off arm hanging out of his candy bag. Brooks has his own truck and drove the other two grandkids over to our house. He is their chaperone for the night. As soon as the kids pass by the old oak tree, Weston pops from behind, growling and howling and chases the kids around the yard. Brooks suddenly stops, turns around, and stares at the werewolf. He is protecting his two siblings. Weston pulls his werewolf head off, and Brooks is shocked to see his grandpa. Caroline and Rylan gather around Weston, and they give him reluctant hugs.

"You scared me, Papa," says Caroline as she swings her hand to hit Weston on the butt.

"Ow," he says, still laughing.

"That's not funny," says Brooks staring into Weston's eyes.

"I thought it was funny," says Weston.

Rylan stands tall and says, "Not funny, bro." He tries to be the cool one.

"Brooks, you did good trying to protect your brother and sister!" I yell.

"Sorry, I scared y'all. When you get older, you can scare your grandkids," says Weston.

I stand in the doorway to the house, recording the whole thing on my cell phone. I can't wait to show the video to their mom and dad. The kids laugh and then come to the door for their treats. I have already made them special bags of candy and threw in some money for each of them, so they are happy. They load back into Brooks' truck, strap on their seatbelts, and off they go, waving goodbye from the rolled-down truck windows.

"Bye, y'all have fun!" I yell. Weston hides behind the oak tree, and I go back to the front door of the house to wait on our next visitors.

Chapter Eighteen

The Friday after Thanksgiving, we Beach Girls meet for Black Friday shopping and breakfast. During breakfast, we plan a Christmas brunch at my house as I inform the girls that there is no update on our case.

Elle says, "I sent the two hairs of the deceased to the DNA Heritage Corporation. I used one of their DNA breakdown kits. It should take about eight weeks or maybe longer for me to get the results back; I really have no idea about how long it will take. I sent it in under the name of Jonathan Doeman?" We all laugh at that as Elle's husband is a big hunter of deer, and the name 'Doeman' is a play on words about his hunting.

I ask, "Mary Beth, have you heard more from Snoop Dog about the murder?"

"No name on the murder victim yet. They still have not located the drug dealer for the marijuana. Snoop Dog says she will let me know if they find out the name of the victim," says Mary Beth.

"Did she mention Detective Franks?" I ask, raising my eyebrows in thought.

"Snoop Dog did say that Franks is drinking a lot more and that her neighbor saw him drunk at the Red Bird Lounge Friday night. The barkeeper took his car keys and called for an Uber driver to take him home. He was slurring his words and wobbling," says Mary Beth.

"What a sleaze," I say.

"I wonder what his deal is," says Elle.

On a Saturday afternoon during the first week of December, I get a phone call from Nancy. "We have to talk privately," she says impatiently. "Are you somewhere where you can talk freely?" she adds.

"Wait, I'll go out by the pool; Weston is watching football," I say.

The weather outside is still in the seventies during the day and high fifties at night. It is a perfect evening for sitting by the pool. Wearing a cream-colored, long sweater and brown leggings with my brown booties, I walk to the table outside by the pool, sit on one of the two lounge chairs and lean back against the soft cushion.

"Okay, what's up?" I ask.

Nancy begins, "I thought I recognized the bearded guy's picture, and I did. He is number six on the FBI's Most Wanted list. He has warrants in New York and Florida for murder! I want to contact my FBI friend in

Jacksonville and let her know what you and the others saw at the Sea Glass House."

"Hold on a minute; let's think this through. I guess I was right about that guy. He must be a hitman," I say, a little nervous.

"His name is James Kilroy," says Nancy. "It appears that he has only been on the FBI's list for a couple of months. Someone in the FBI is looking for him, and he is dangerous," she adds.

"Alright, here is what you do. Contact your FBI friend and give her my cell number. Have her call me, and I will set up a time and place to meet. Do not tell her about our file; only tell her about the picture. OK?" I ask. "By the way, what's her name?" I add.

"What file?" asks Nancy.

"Nothing, forget about it," I reply. There is no need to get Nancy more involved at this time.

"Her name is Rachel Watts. I've known her since middle school, and we have kept in touch. She is a straight shooter, and you can trust her. Sara, please be careful. This guy is dangerous. I worry about the investigating you girls do," says Nancy.

"We're smart women, don't worry your pretty little head about us," I say confidently.

"Love you guys," says Nancy as she hangs up the phone.

It just happens to be a Saturday evening. I make a conference call to the Beach Girls, knowing they will all be home. We pretty much keep in touch with each other either on the phone or texting at least twice a week.

"Hey girls, I just got a call from Nancy, and this is important. Are you all where no one but you can hear me?" I ask.

"Yes," they all say in unison, and I continue.

"Nancy has identified the bearded man from the Octagon House, and you are not going to believe it. He is number six on the FBI's Most Wanted list. His name is James Kilroy. He has warrants for him in New York and Florida for murder for hire. He also has warrants for resisting and aggravated arrest."

"Oh my Lord, I should have looked at those pictures on the wall of the post office. They are all over the post office on every bulletin board. I have been at the post office way too long; I just ignore them and walk on by," says Mary Beth shaking her head.

"No way!" shockingly exclaims Elle.

"You were right, Sara," says Cici. "You said you thought it was a hitman; we just didn't know he was staying next door to the Sea Glass House," she adds.

"Listen, Nancy has a friend in Jacksonville who is an FBI agent. Her name is Rachel Watts, and Nancy has known her for a long time. I told

Nancy it was ok to give her my phone number. When she calls, I will set a day and time to meet with her. Nancy is really worried about us; I could tell it in her voice. I told her not to worry about us and that we would not do anything stupid. Please, please, please keep this information to yourself. No one else needs to know anything," I say.

I wait a few seconds and then say, "Ok, we need a meeting place." I gaze around, looking at the water rippling in the pool, waiting for a reply.

Lizzy responds, "We can meet out at my farm in MacClenny. It will be safe there and it is secure. You know there is only one way down the dirt road off of SR220, and that Is the only way out too. I have cameras connected to the roof around the outside of the house, and I have a safe room if we need it. Everyone will be well protected out there. Also, Agent Watts won't have a difficult time finding the farmhouse."

Cici breathes heavily and states, "I think we should tell the agent about the murder, too."

"According to Snoop Dog, as of yesterday, they still have not identified the murder victim," says Mary Beth. "There isn't that much to tell," she adds.

"Ok, right now, I think Cici, Lizzy, and I should meet with Agent Watts. We will give her the information we have from the day Cici discovered the murder victim until the time we saw the bearded man. Until we know that she is on the level and can be trusted, we will keep the case file hidden. What do y'all say?" I ask.

"Agree," they all say.

Eight o'clock that night, Agent Watts calls my cell phone. "Yes?" I ask.

"Mrs. Springs? Sara Springs?" the agent asks.

"Yes, how can I help you?" I ask, not being overly helpful.

"I hope I can help relieve you ladies of some stress. This is FBI Agent Watts. I received a call from a mutual friend who informed me that you have some valuable information that may be helpful on one of our cases. Is there any place private that we can meet?" she asks.

"Yes, my friends and I will meet you tomorrow morning at Elizabeth Mackie's farm The address is 54628 Honeydew Lane, MacClenny, Florida. There is a gray house next to the dirt drive that will take you to the house. Please be there at ten in the morning. We have something interesting to show you," I say and quickly hang up the phone. The less said on phones, the better.

I call Lizzy and Cici, "The meeting is set for tomorrow at Lizzy's farmhouse," I say. "Let's try to get there by nine thirty," I add.

"Ok. I will make coffee and Danish cherry rolls," says Lizzy.

"Don't go through too much trouble," says Cici. "I will bring you a jar of my freshly made blueberry jam I will bring blueberry scones too; I make them with almond flour, honey, and fresh blueberries," she adds, always the nutritionist.

Chapter Nineteen

Cici and I arrive at the farm at nine thirty.

"Are you nervous?" I question Lizzy and Cici.

"Not really. I have been looking out the windows since seven this morning and haven't seen anything out of the ordinary so far. You know police, judges, and feds don't scare me. I have testified a few times in my life. I don't have anything to worry about; I keep to myself, except when I am around y'all," says Lizzy smiling.

"Don't blame your bad self for being around us," I respond, smiling.

Cici adds, "Well, it has been long since I smoked a joint, being a nurse and all the 'ree-stric-tions'. Heck no, I am not scared. I have never smoked a joint in my life!" Cici laughs, and Lizzy and I laugh with her.

"I don't think she will make us take a drug test," I say, laughing. "Ok, I think we are ready," I say, walking over to the kitchen window.

Lizzy takes three coffee cups out of the cabinet and three Coke Zeros out of the refrigerator. "What do you want, coffee or coke," she says.

"I'll take Coke Zero, please," I say.

"I'll just have ice water, thank you," says Cici.

I keep watching outside while the other ladies munch cherry Danishes and blueberry scones. I spot a black SUV coming down the road and turn to the girls.

"Do all FBI agents drive black SUVs?" I ask, grinning. I turn back to the window.

I watch as the agent parks the government automobile and opens the SUV door. Agent Watts is a svelte, 5 feet 9 inches tall woman in her forties. Her auburn hair is cut above her ears and parted on the right, with little wisps of hair lying on her forehead. You can tell she uses a lot of hair products by the way her hair stands atop her scalp. Her hairstyle is very appealing and modern for today's woman. She is wearing a dark blue pants suit with a white tee and black work boots. Her ears are adorned with medium-sized diamond studs. I can see her holstered gun beneath her jacket as she slowly walks toward the door. Her body moves with command; she looks badass. She steps up on the large wooden porch and rings the bell. Lizzy opens the beautiful oak door with side windows and asks, "Agent Watts?"

"Yes, and you are?" the agent asks, looking past Lizzy into the dining area of the open floor-plan house. Typical FBI agent; they are always nosey.

"I am Lizzy, Elizabeth Mackie. This is Cici Downs and you have already spoken with Sara Springs," Lizzy answers. "Please come in," Lizzy adds, motioning the agent into the living area.

"Would you like something to drink?" I ask.

"Yes, water would be great. It is a rather long drive from Jacksonville Beach to MacClenny and a bit warm," she says, smiling.

"So, you live out at the beach?" I ask.

"Yes, I grew up in Jacksonville and love the beach. After I started working for the FBI, I moved out there," she says.

I hand her the glass of water as Lizzy leads us to the large, wooden dining table with tall, cowhide leather chairs. Her house is styled with a mixture of farmlife and cattle rancher furnishings. The house has a huge sunroom which allows the sunshine into the room, and the beautiful blue walls give the room an air of openness.

"I believe you have a picture of a bearded man that you ladies took at the Matanzas Inlet. You were there for a Beach Girls' weekend, right?" Agent Watts asks, focusing on the task at hand.

"Yes. Before we give you the picture, there is something we need to tell you. Cici, do you want to start first?" I ask, looking at Cici.

"Ok. When we were at the Sea Glass House, I decided to take my canoe out into the inlet that Friday morning. I went down to the dock, picked up my oars, and stepped into the canoe. The canoe started rocking and I fell in head first, getting my body soaked. When I came back up, I looked under the dock and saw a body looking at me. At first, I couldn't tell what it was because it was covered with seaweed. I am a nurse, and my first inclination was to drag him out of the water and check his pulse. I grabbed him and pulled him into the canoe. I knew he was dead, but I tried to resuscitate him. Sara was watching from her bedroom balcony overlooking the dock and the Matanzas Inlet; she ran down here to the dock. She called Lizzy to have her contact the police. I stayed with the body," says Cici.

I add, "I was just sitting on the balcony when I saw Cici fall into the water and pop back up out of the inlet. She was acting strange, so I grabbed my phone and ran down to where she was in the canoe. The wind was blowing slightly and vultures were swirling in a circle high above the boat. I saw the man's body lying in the canoe, and the look on Cici's face was frightening. When Cici shook her head and came to her senses, she told me the man was dead. I called Lizzy back at the house since her name was on our lease agreement and asked her to call the police."

"I called the Flager Police Department and then the rental agent, Mya from Beach Rentals of Florida," Lizzy says. "That's when the rest of us ran down the dock to Cici and Sara."

"It must have been twenty or so minutes before the police arrived. Detective Franks and his partner came up the stairs to the house. By this time, the other ladies had rushed back to the house," I say.

"Ok, I can check on that later," says the agent.

"Well, here is the picture I took the night after the body was found," I state, turning over the picture and handing it to the agent.

"I thought I saw someone in the Octagon House the afternoon Cici found the dead man. That night I was looking from the bedroom window upstairs and saw someone walking around outside the house. I motioned for Sara to come have a look and heard a large pickup truck pull up. The bearded man got into the passenger side of the truck," said Lizzy.

"I took the picture with my cell phone," I say. "There was just enough light from the truck's inside cab to get a clear picture. I did not see the driver as he had his back toward us," I add.

"Yes, it was the same face I saw in the window that afternoon," said Lizzy.

"Have you ladies ever seen the man before or afterwards?" the agent asks.

"Yes," Lizzy and I replied.

"We did see him a couple of nights later. He somehow appeared again at the Octagon House; we did not see any automobile return to the house during the day. Although that day, we were not looking for anyone. He was looking around the dock at the Octagon House and walking along the shore of the Inlet. We had been out at the beach most of the day and were drained from the sun," I say.

"Listen, ladies, I do not want the Beach Girls to do any more investigating. Nancy has told me a little about your investigations, and even though I am impressed with your case-solving skills, this James Kilroy is one dangerous man. From what we know, he is wanted for the murders of two witnesses in a New York Crime Boss federal case and another murder in Miami, Florida, related to a drug cartel. Our friend Nancy is very worried about you ladies, and I know you don't want to worry her," said Watts.

"We will stay out of your way, Agent Watts, and leave the case to you. Please let us know what happens after you catch him," I say. We were not about to tell her of the hair samples, concrete or anything else.

The agent gets up, places her water glass in the kitchen sink and walks toward the door. "Nice meeting you ladies, and I will be back in touch," she says. "I can see why Nancy thinks so highly of you," she adds, opening the door and moving toward her SUV.

After she leaves, I ask, "Well, what do y'all think about Agent Watts?"

Lizzy says, "I like her, but I am not ready to tell her everything. I think we should do some research on this James Kilroy."

"I agree. Next Saturday is our Christmas brunch at my house; we can discuss it then. Weston is going Christmas shopping, so he will be gone all day," I say.

"I'll text the girls to make sure that they will all be there," says Lizzy.

"Yall, this is some crazy stuff. I bet James keeled (in that southern drawl) the man that I found. Don't y'all?" asks Cici.

"Yes, I do," I say.

Chapter Twenty

My house is all decorated for Christmas, and it looks like the Christmas spirit has taken over every room. I have wreaths on the doors, a lite garland attached to the fireplace mantel, red and green comforters and pillow shams on all the beds, and a Christmas shower curtain with holly berry hangers. I love this time of the year.

I busy myself cooking my vegetable beef soup loaded with carrots, potatoes, green beans, corn, tomatoes, onions, fresh garlic cloves, and ground chuck; this is Weston's favorite winter meal. I think to myself, "Have we gotten into something that we can't get out of? No. We are good at investigating, and we are grown women who can take care of ourselves," I say. Right then, I decide to tell Weston about the man we found at Sea Glass House, nothing more.

Weston listens and says, "Baby, I know you girls are good at what y'all do, but please be careful. I don't know what I would do without you. How about we go to the target range for a little shooting practice?"

"I'm fine. You know I know how to shoot; I just don't like guns," I say.

We kiss, and I head to the computer in my home office. The office is small with an antique oak secretary desk and a laptop computer. I sit down in my comfy leather office chair and take a stack of essays out of my briefcase. I have a ton of grading to do before the Christmas break. I pull out the essays of my 11th grade English III class and begin to grade papers. The essays are not too bad, but after about two hours of reading papers on "Why Cell Phones Should Be Allowed in School", I am ready for a glass of wine and chocolate!

Saturday morning, I get up early to prepare for the Christmas brunch. All the girls are bringing a dish; lucky for us, they are great cooks. I prepare my Danish cheese made with crescent rolls, cream cheese, vanilla flavoring, and powdered sugar. Once baked, I add a can of cooked pie cherries to the center of the pastry and finish it off with a sprinkling of white power sugar. It looks so pretty, like a Christmas wreath. I perk some Starbucks Christmas coffee and pour some half-and-half milk into the Depression glass creamer. I grab the sugar out of the pantry and pour some into my Depression glass sugar dish. I also prepare my bacon-wrapped water chestnuts with grape jelly and barbeque sauce. The girls love the chestnuts. Anything wrapped in bacon, southern girls will eat. Well, we will eat the bacon. I save a few for Weston and place his paper plate into the microwave.

Lizzy is the first to arrive with her warm pecan pie muffins. Mary Beth is right behind her, coming through the doorway and heading to the kitchen. She is ready to scramble some eggs and fry some bacon. Cici drives up in her new car and grabs her angel biscuits with the fresh strawberry jam out of the back seat. Elle arrives a few minutes later and brings the champagne and orange juice for mimosas.

"Sara, your Christmas tree is beautiful. I need you to decorate mine; I just can't seem to get all those decorations together. Mine looks like someone threw on some lights, bulbs and garland. You can hardly see the colored bulbs on it," says Elle.

"I saw you decorated the guest bedroom this year," says Cici. I love the Christmas bedspread you have in that room, and the little natural trees on the nightstands are adorable. You know, sometimes plain is more beautiful than all those fancy trees. I have a real tree at my house. My grandson and I went into the woods behind our neighborhood and cut it down right by ourselves. Have you been taking your supplements like I told you?" she adds.

After brunch, we head into the den to play our annual "White Elephant; Gift Exchange" game. This year I asked all the girls to bring a gag gift. Each lady drew a number out of a Christmas gift bag for their turn at selecting a gift. Elle chose number one. All the gifts are situated next to the fireplace. She examines each present carefully, finally picks one, and returns to her seat to open it.

Elle opens the gift and pulls out a knitted moose head covering. The antlers on the moose light up with red and green lights. She puts it on her head and says, "I wonder if I can catch a male moose with this hat?"

I laugh and answer, "It is a male moose hat!"

"Well, I like that hat and might just pick it when it is my turn," says Cici.

"Number two!" I yell.

Mary Beth gets up and looks at Elle's hat before moving to the other gifts for her selection. "I do love the hat, but I think I will choose this one," she says, picking up a medium-sized box with gold paper and a red bow. She opens her box and pulls out a red and white striped apron with candy canes glued to the front of the apron. "I don't even cook!" she squeals.

"Number three!" I yell. "Oh wait, I am number three," I laugh and get up from my chair. There are only three gifts left, and one is from me. I take a long look at the hat and the apron and then pick a small package from the gift group. I open my bag, and inside it is a roll of Christmas toilet paper. "Hey, Weston and I could use this," I say, holding up the paper and laughing.

"Look again. There is something else in there," says Cici.

I look again, and a small item is wrapped in white tissue paper at the bottom of the bag. I unwrap the item and ask, "What is this?"

"It is a night light for the toilet. It comes on when you sit down and can change colors," says Cici.

"That's cool; I can use one of them. It is so dark in the house when I get up at night to go to the bathroom," says Elle.

"Me too," says Lizzy.

"You are not getting mine," I say, laughing.

"Number four, you are next," I say.

Lizzy gets up from her seat next to me and moseys over to Mary Beth, "I will take the apron, please. I look good in candy canes, and I do cook," she says with a grin on her face.

Mary Beth frowns and heads over to get the small box wrapped in red and green striped paper. She takes it back to her seat and gently removes the wrapping paper from the box as if it is going to explode. "It is not a bomb," I say.

"You never know with you girls," says Mary Beth as she continues to remove the paper from around the gift. She opens the top of the small box and starts laughing. "I know I said I wanted a man. But, I meant a live one," she says, holding up a small statute of a well-built, naked man, a copy of the statute of David.

"He is fine, though," adds Elle.

We all get a good laugh watching Mary Beth examine the small statute. "Number five!" I yell.

Cici stands up and removes the statute from Mary Beth's hand. "I just want to getter a closer look," she says, and we all laugh louder. She hands the statute back to Mary Beth. "I want the moose cap; I will wear it at the hospital to uplift the staff. They love my quirkiness, and besides, it looks good on me," she adds, placing the cap on her head.

Elle now has to either select one of our gifts or pick the last gift. I know what it is because I bought it. I wrapped it in a piece of old, stained cloth and tied it with a piece of red yarn. It was the ugliest gift wrapping in the whole group of gifts. Elle picks up the gift and looks at me with a "what the heck" look. She takes off the yarn and cloth slowly. She removes the lid from the box, looks at the gift, and laughs out loud. Inside, she finds a pair of fuzzy, nonskid deer socks with antlers and a red nose that lights up. I also bought a pair of doe socks with white spots that light up too. I did not want the male deer to feel alone. "Well, I guess Santa wanted me to have a pet this year!" she squeals.

After our gift game, we sit around the dining table and begin our discussion on the Sea Glass case.

"Girls, there is something else we need to tell y'all before we get too involved," says Lizzy. "Sara and I, when we were at the beach, went snooping around the other two houses. Remember when Sara and I took the canoe out for diving and snorkeling? Well, we found out where the man's body came from. The end of the rope was tied to a concrete pier connected to the dock of the Octagon House. I retrieved a piece of the concrete sludge and sent it to a company that examines concrete. It will take a while for us to get the results, but these chemists can tell us the exact chemical makeup of the concrete. We didn't want to mention it to you at the beach with everything else happening, so we waited until today. Since we have met with Agent Watts, we wanted to get everything out in the open," Lizzy explains.

"When do you think you will get the results back?" asks Elle.

"I am not really sure; it will take a few months. The process is complicated, but I do expect the scientists to complete their research and have results by the end of March or the beginning of April," says Lizzy.

"What about the DNA? Any results?" I ask Elle.

"No, no news yet. Mr. Doeman's ancestry has not been identified. Wouldn't it be something if he is related to one of us? He could be related to Ryan. That would explain a lot," says Elle laughing. "I truly love that old man," she adds.

"Please don't say that he could be related to one of us," says Lizzy with a contemplative look.

"What would be funny is if the guy ends up being related to Nancy," I say with a grin.

"That would be funny," says Elle.

"When we met with the FBI agent, Cici told her about finding the deceased and her interaction with Detective Franks. The agent said she would look into that situation and talk with Franks. Lizzy and I informed her about the bearded man and gave her a copy of the picture. We did not tell her about the hairs or the case file we have," I continue.

"Agent Watts indicated that she will let us know what happens and for us to stay out of this," said Lizzy. "We agreed but still didn't tell her about the rope or concrete. I think she misunderstood our depth of investigating."

"Maybe you should tell her everything," says Mary Beth. "Snoop Dog says that the cops still have no leads," she adds.

"The Flagler County detectives should have found the information already, and they can fill the agent in. Let the cops do their jobs. After all, they still haven't found out who the dead man is or where the bales of the pot came from," I say sternly.

"All right, other than getting back the details of the cement and hairs, there is not much to investigate," says Elle.

"Right, at least not yet," I whisper.

We drink a toast to the Beach Girls and Nancy since she is in New York. "Merry Christmas, Beach Girls," we raise our crystal glasses filled to the rims with mimosas and toast.

Chapter Twenty-One

At the end of December, Weston, Pop, and I decide to take a trip back to Biloxi, Mississippi, for a little gambling. The casinos are always decorated so beautifully at Christmas and give away more money during the holiday season. We travel the same route on Interstate 10, stopping at Cracker Barrel in Tallahassee for breakfast: eggs, grits, bacon, and whole grain toast/biscuits. Of course, my southern men get sausage patties. While bacon is the choice of most southern people, pork of any kind is a breakfast commodity.

Another couple of rest stops before Biloxi, and my excitement increases as I begin to shift and wiggle in my seat. I love the lights and music in the casinos. The billboards along the interstate flash, announcing big giveaways and prizes. When we turn off the highway, I see the Scarlet Pearl Casino sign beckoning me; I get my money ready. Weston stops at the Scarlet Pearl and parks on the second floor of the self-parking garage. Weston, Pop, and I enter the casino's elevator and push the button for the first floor. We exit the elevator and make our way to the cashier's counter of the casino. Every time I go gambling, I have to get new club cards. For some reason, I can't seem to keep them.

We stand in line looking out toward the slot machines and see an older man push a button on the Cashman slot machine. The wheels turn round and round, and the Cashman lands on the screen. The bells begin to roar as the machine lights up the words "Big Winner". The man just won five hundred and thirty dollars.

"Wow, did you see that? I hope we have that kind of luck," I say.

"That guy was playing five dollars each time he pressed the button on the slot machine," says Pop.

"Well, that won't be me," I reply.

I get my new card and check the kiosk for any freebies. No free gifts, but I do have fifty dollars in slot money and head to the 'Slap the Sharks' game. I sit down in the comfortable chair in front of the slot machine and push my rewards card into the slot. At first, it refuses to take my card. After a couple of tries, it lights up green, and I transfer the fifty dollars into my slot. I use my fifty dollars in less than thirty minutes. You win some, and you lose some.

I walk around the casino, looking at the decorations and admire all the beautiful trees and wreaths. The Scarlet Pearl has six-foot wreaths with sheer, scarlet and gold ribbons circling the green Christmas wreaths. Gigantic pearls which shimmer in the lights hang from the ceiling as if the ocean was gently flowing overhead. It is so intoxicating and festive. Everywhere you look, people are smiling and pointing to the ceiling. Many are taking pictures and videos with their cameras. I go into the Roasted Bean coffee shop and order a ginger coffee and a peppermint sugar cookie. I need a little caffeine to keep me awake for the next few hours as it is going to be a long day after traveling seven hours. But who cares; we are gambling and on vacation!

After a couple of hours, Weston, Pop, and I meet up at the entrance to the elevators of the self-parking area to drive to the Island View Casino, where we always stay. It is only a few miles away as we take a beautiful drive along the coastline. Upon arrival at the casino and hotel, we turn the keys over to the valet and remove our luggage from the car's trunk. We roll our luggage into the line for check-in. Pop, Weston, and I wait about fifteen minutes in line to check into our room. In front of us are a tall, handsome cowboy and his group of friends registering for their rooms. The cowboy must be someone special since the manager and several bellhops load their luggage onto carriers.

"Oh my goodness, it is Tim MacMadison and his band," I whisper to Weston.

"I think you are right. He and his band are playing at the Island View tomorrow night in the auditorium. Do you want to go to the concert?" asks Weston giving me a thoughtful look.

I just love Tim and his wife, Hope. They are both great singers. I have seen them before in concert at the Jacksonville Center of the Arts. Tim slowly turns around, facing us, and apologizes for our delay. I give him a big smile as Weston reaches out and shakes his hand.

"No problem. I enjoy your music very much," says Weston.

"Me too. I love to hear your wife sing," I say with a smile.

Tim and his band follow the bellhops to the elevators, enter and disappear.

We finally register and have a bellhop deliver our luggage to the room. Pop, Weston, and I are hungry as we have not had anything since breakfast. Well, I had ginger coffee and a sugar cookie from the Roasted Bean. We head to the Island View buffet since Pop still has enough points on his card for at least ten free buffets. We get a table near the seafood station and look around the dining room to see what everyone has on their plates. The burly man at the table next to ours has a loaded plate of boiled shrimp, a plate of fried chicken and one filled with mashed potatoes. "I guess he is hungry," I say, grinning.

A woman sitting at a table in front of ours has a plate of desserts: pie, cake, cobbler, and fudge. "She likes her sweets," I whisper to Pop.

"Looks that way," says Pop. The place is divided into several sections: Southern food, seafood, Oriental, Southwestern and barbeque, Italian pizza, salads and desserts. I select the seared, blackened tilapia, boiled shrimp and shrimp jambalaya. I enjoy my spicy seafood since it is healthy; just ask Cici. I make myself a lettuce, tomatoes, cucumber and citrus salad with Thousand Island dressing. I add some grated cheese and walk back to the table. Weston has a large plate of crab legs, melted butter, potato au gratin, and a side salad of lettuce and tomatoes. Pop returns to the table with a spring roll, a slice of pepperoni pizza, fried catfish, cheese grits, and a small fruit bowl. It looks like his plate has gone on a world tour. We do love to eat; it runs in my family.

The Island View's Christmas decorating theme is all about the sea. The huge green wreaths are wrapped in ribbons of coral, aqua, sea green, and white. Attached to the wreaths are large sea shells: conch shells, star fish, and huge pearls. Some of the pearls lie in large clam shells attached to the wreaths. Opaque glitter has been gently tossed onto the wreaths to give them a sparkle as if they were just picked up from a sandy ocean floor. Add to that a twenty-five feet tree with the same décor; the place was magical. Christmas is an amazing time of the year, and these places spare no expense. Today in the casino, they are giving away Christmas ornaments and candy canes.

After we eat and walk around the casino a little, Pop leaves us to go to the poker tables. Weston and I walk around a little more before finding two slot machines open next to each other. We get a drink from the waitress who serves the patrons playing the slot machines. Weston has a beer and I have a glass of wine. We play a few dollars in the machines and then decide to get our awards' cards.

Weston and I walk up to the Island Views Club counter, and I get my new player's card from the cashier's window. I check the kiosk for my freebies and kiosk games. Today's game is to select one of the Christmas bulbs on the kiosk screen for an award. I select the blue bulb, as blue is my favorite color and win six times.

I don't have any free play, so I put a hundred-dollar bill into the Ragin Cagin Gator slot machine and play for a couple of hours. I haven't lost anything, but I am tired from the long trip. I find Weston at the bar playing a poker machine and sidle up next to him.

"Hey baby, I'm tired. I am going to the room," I whisper into his ear.

"I'm coming with you," Weston replies as he gets up from his seat and prints out his ticket from the slot machine. We walk over to the cash retrieval machine located in the middle of the casino floor. Weston places his ticket into the slot and receives his cash. I place my ticket into the machine and retrieve my hundred-dollar bill.

Our suite this time is a lovely, two-bedroom suite with a king bed in each bedroom and separate bathrooms. We have a kitchenette and a small living area with a gray, soft sofa and armchair sitting between the bedrooms. The coffee table is the kind that rises up to the height of a dining table. A large, wide-screen television hangs above the mantel of the electric fireplace. The room is of the perfect size. Besides, I can still hear when Pop enters the room, so I don't have to worry about him. Weston and I are in bed before Pop every night, but it is hard for me to fall asleep. I wish I had his energy.

We take the elevator located right outside the reservation desk up to our floor and enter our room. I check for calls on the phone. After watching one of our regular programs, Weston and I change into our pjs to sleep. Weston is an early riser and gets up by seven o'clock every day. He gets at least ten hours of sleep every night, which makes me jealous. I know I won't be able to sleep until Pop comes in, so I decide to read my latest Tom Clancy novel. I hear him slipping into his room around one o'clock. Relieved that he is alright and safe in his bed, I place my novel on the nightstand and gently nod off to sleep.

Chapter Twenty-Two

The next morning, we get out of bed around eight o'clock. Weston has already gone down for coffee. I am sure he has already placed a couple of bets on tonight's football game. I hear Pop moving around in his room and decide to change. A few minutes later, Weston returns with delicious-smelling coffee. We gather in the shared living area and watch the weather forecast on the TV while drinking our coffee. After a few minutes, we head out toward the elevators. Pop, Weston, and I have a full day of gambling waiting for us.

"Hey, Pop, you want to go to the show tonight? Tim MacMadison and Hope are singing?" Weston asks.

"Yeah, they are really good; you will like them. They sing country music," I say.

"No, you go and enjoy. I am going to play cards tonight. I am up six hundred dollars and don't want my luck to wear out," he chuckles.

"Ok," Weston says, walking to the entertainment desk to purchase our tickets. The lady behind the desk asks Weston for his name.

"Yeah, baby, we are going to the concert," I tell myself.

"Sir, I have an envelope for you from Mr. MacMadison," says the lady.

"We'll get the car brought to the front door from the valet service," I say, heading out the door of the Island View with Pop.

Weston opens the envelope, which contains two concert tickets. Not just any tickets, but the second row in front of the stage in the VIP section tickets. The little note from Tim read, "Enjoy tonight." We are overwhelmed.

Pop and I meet Weston out front of the lobby by the car.

"Where to, guys?" I ask.

"The Waffle House," says Pop.

We are all a little hungry, and Pop likes their smothered fries. We stop at the nearest Waffle House, only a couple of blocks from the hotel. I order whole wheat toast and scrambled eggs. Weston has scrambled eggs, sausage patties, hash browns, and biscuits. Pop has the same but adds cheese, onions, and tomatoes to his hash browns. We order coffee and water to go with our meal.

"Guess what? Tim gave us two free tickets to the second row in the VIP section of tonight's concert. It is already a winning day," says Weston.

“Whoo! Hoo!” I yell. “We are finally VIPs!” I yell excitedly. After we eat, Weston pays the bill, and we get back into the car.

“Where to Pop?” I ask.

I usually drive while we are in Biloxi so the guys can concentrate on the beautiful views, allowing them to gather their cards and money before going into the casinos. I am impatient when it comes to going somewhere, so I have to drive.

“The Beaurivage,” says Pop.

The Beaurivage Casino and Hotel is fabulous. The casino’s Christmas décor is always traditional with red and green and always snowmen. The spruce Christmas tree must be at least thirty feet tall with large white lights and red satin bulbs hanging from its snow-covered limbs.

Along the pathway to the casino are five feet in circumference, shiny red and gold bulbs placed randomly throughout the walkways. A couple of the large Christmas bulbs are placed underneath the tree, along with Christmas presents wrapped in gold and red paper. Next to a small, snowed-topped tree forest, surrounding both sides of the large entranceway hall, are new red Cadillac SUVs. These cars will be given away on New Year’s Eve. It is a shame we won’t be here that long. Holly wreaths and garlands of red and white ribbon adorn the stairs and staircases. Christmas music is playing through the speakers from the parking garage all the way to the casino entrance. We stop next to the large Christmas balls, and Weston takes a picture of Pop and me. This picture is a nice memory I will have to display in our house.

Once we arrive at the casino, we hear rock music blaring from the sound system. Pop and I do a little wiggling to the beat of the music. Flashing lights and rock n roll, I am ready to go. The security guard checks our ID before we enter the room. The casino has security throughout the building to ensure the safety of its guests. There are several restrooms on each casino floor, and they are constantly being cleaned by custodians. The chairs next to the slot machines are placed underneath the machine overhangs as each person moves from one seat to another. This is done regularly to keep patrons from getting tripped as they move around to the different areas of the casino.

Once again, I head to the cashier's window to get my new player's card. This is getting tiresome. So, from now on, I am going to put my cards in the glove compartment of my SUV. I head to the kiosk to check on freebies, games, and slot money. This time, I get lucky and receive a free Christmas ornament ticket and one hundred dollars on the slots. I walk around, up and down the aisles, checking to see if there are any new slot machines that I have yet to play. I look down a long aisle that appears to go on and on. There, at the end of the aisle, is a new slot machine, "Shake the Apple Tree." I hear it calling my name in my head and hustle down the aisle before anyone else can get to the machine. I place my hundred-dollar bill into the money receptor. Two hundred dollars are waiting for me to bet as I add my own hundred. I am ready to place my hands on that screen and shake that apple tree. I use up the free money within thirty minutes and play the game for about an hour more using my own money. I haven't lost my hundred, so I decide to bet five dollars each time on the same machine. I don't usually bet more than two dollars; I am a cheap gambler. Today, however, I am going big. I have a good feeling about this machine.

All of a sudden, the machine gives me the "shake the tree" sign, and I get ready. Bam, I grab that tree on the large screen and start shaking those apples. My hands are rapidly moving back and forth across the screen. The apples start flying off the tree, and the sound from the machine gets louder and louder.

Weston comes up behind me, baffled, and says, "What's going on?"

I keep shaking that tree; I want all the apples. At once, I notice that one of the apples is golden. I begin to feel a rush flow through me. I shake the apple tree like a mad woman. When the screen stops, and my hands slowly remove themselves from the screen, I look up to see lights flashing and people gathering around me. I knew I must have won something, but little did I know. A woman and man dressed in black suits and white dress shirts come up to me.

The man says, "Congratulations, you have just won the 'Shake the Apple Tree' jackpot. The golden apple is worth fifty thousand dollars; with your other winnings, you have won fifty thousand and one hundred dollars."

I start doing my happy dance bouncing on my feet and screaming, "Yes, Yes, Yes!"

Weston is still staring at the slot machine; he can't move. I have to wait a few minutes for the woman to get my big check. They ask me for permission to take my picture with the check. I agree, and when the big check arrives, I straighten my blue silk blouse and put on a big smile. Nothing like this has ever happened to me before, and I am super excited. Weston is still dumbfounded as we follow the officials back to the cashier's counter. I notice another official-looking man in a dark suit and tie standing near the counter. He looks at me and says, "I am with the Internal Revenue Service; I will be taking Uncle Sam's part of your winnings." He doesn't even smile or say congratulations.

Weston says, "Take what belongs to the IRS. The rest is fun money anyways." That's Weston always straight to the point, even though the money is my winnings.

After taxes, I receive a large sum of money and feel high on life. First, I head to the nearest ATM and deposit my check. I still had a few bucks with me and needed all this to sink in before I went on a spending spree. I am pragmatic, after all.

Weston kisses me and says, "Good job, baby." He heads back to the poker bar, orders a beer, and I start searching the tables for Pop.

I walk down one aisle after another. All I see are a bunch of gray-haired men with red shirts. Before the trip, I purchased a new red shirt for Pop to wear in order to make it easier for me to find him. These casinos are large, and ninety percent of the casino visitors have white hair, like Pop. Little did I know that all the silver foxes would be wearing red shirts for the day. It took me a while to locate him sitting at a table with five other players. Pop is sitting at the high roller poker table and in front of him is a big stack of chips. It looks like he is doing pretty well for himself.

I lean over and whisper into his right ear, "Pop, I just won fifty thousand on the 'Shake the Apple Tree'."

Pop's head snaps around, and he gives me a big smile as he says, "Way to go."

"How are you doing?" I ask, smiling back at him.

"Not bad," he says, turning back to the table.

Pop likes to focus on his cards. He lays down his cards and wins the pot: three hundred dollars. I smile and walk away, leaving him to his gambling.

I decide to take a look at the Winner Circle in the casino and see who else has been winning. I stop in my tracks; I can't believe what I see. There hanging against a tan wall in the Winner Circle area, is a four feet by six feet picture of our murder victim. Apparently, before the man was killed, he had been gambling at the Beaurivage. Here he was, Sonny Manuzco, smiling and holding a ten-thousand-dollar check. The plaque on the picture indicates Sonny is from New York, a New York native apparently. I grab my cell phone and take a quick photo of the plaque and one of the entire picture and plaque. I still can't believe that I just happened to see this picture. Sonny even has on his pinkie ring. I walk back to Weston at the bar and say, "Weston, please come with me for a minute."

Weston asks, "Ok, baby. Is anything wrong?"

"I am not sure," I say, grabbing his hand and walking back to the Winner Circle.

Once there, I point to Manuzco's picture. "That is the dead guy we found at the beach, Sonny Manuzco."

"Oh my God," says Weston and places his arm around me, drawing me close. "What are you going to do?" he asks.

"I really don't want to think about it now," I reply. "I took a picture. I'll figure out what to do when I get back home," I add.

Weston and I meet with Pop and decide to go to lunch and the Hard Rock Casino. Still recovering from the events that morning, I say, "Pop, how is your day going?" I never mention the picture.

Pop replies, "Not as good as yours, but I am up a couple of thousand. Did you pay the IRS man?"

"Yes, he was there waiting for us," I say with a smirk. "Why do they have to be so hateful?"

Pop laughs, "I have paid him a few times myself. I bet he didn't even congratulate you."

"No. What's with that?" I ask.

"I guess since he doesn't get to play, he is not happy with you and me winning," Pop answers. "What are you going to do with your winnings?" he asks as we head to the SUV.

"I have already put the check in the bank and am giving you a couple of thousand for future gambling. Let's just say it is a late Christmas present. You can spend it on our next trip; it doesn't look like you need it this trip. And I am buying us lunch," I say.

"You don't have to give me any of your money, but I will let you buy lunch. I think I will have a T-bone steak about this thick," Pop says, placing his fingers about two inches apart. I love to see Pop joking around. At least, I think he is joking.

"I know you don't want any money; I want you to have the money since you are my gambling buddy," I say, giving Pop a hug.

"Well, thank you," says Pop, returning my hug.

"What are you giving me?" asks Weston with a smile on his face.

"You can go on a fishing trip with your buddies because my Beach Girls are going to New York with me," I say, not letting on that I intend to investigate Sonny Manuzco.

We leave the casino and head back to the Island View Hotel and Casino. Inside the Island View is a quaint, little café, The Starlight Café, which serves southern meals, sandwiches, and burgers. Their french fries come in a separate dinner plate of their own. The restaurant décor is fifty's style with red and black chairs and red tabletop chrome tables.

Pop says, "This place reminds me of the drug store where I grew up. They had a little diner inside that served the best milkshakes."

The hostess leads us to one of the tables. I order the cheeseburger and fries. Weston and Pop order the special for that day, country fried steak, mashed potatoes, and steamed vegetables with a side salad. I take a bite of my cheeseburger, and my taste buds do a little dance in my mouth. "This is the best burger I have ever eaten," I exclaim

We gamble for a few more hours, and Weston and I go to the concert to hear Tim and Hope. We have a good time at the concert and drink a few cocktails. Tim and his wife, Hope, step down from the stage to the VIP area to meet everyone. It was a great night.

The following days were just as wonderful. For the first time, Weston, Pop, and I are all going home winners. Pop won big at the Poker table; Weston hit a few big pots of cash on the slots. It is good to be winners.

Chapter Twenty-Three

On New Year's Eve, the Beach Girls, Weston, and Ryan, Elle's husband, have dinner at Ciao's in Fernandina Beach, Florida. The small town is only twenty-five minutes from my house. Centre Street at the beach lits up with thousands of tiny white lights, making the small tourist town look like a village from the Victorian Days. The red brick buildings touch one another on both sides as if they were hugging. The businesses, shops, and restaurants, along with their sidewalks, are lined with people up and down the street. The shop windows of the buildings are lit with colorful lights; small scenes of Christmas past fill the window displays. Many people are making their way to the marina at the end of the street. Small gas lights sit on each corner, lighting the way to the ocean.

Ciao's restaurant is located in one of the older buildings on Centre Street. The interior is very Italian, with a dark walnut bar in the front room where neighbors and visitors toast one another with their glasses of wine and other spirits. A dining area of wooden tables with white linen table clothes and red napkins completes the scene. The atmosphere is romantic, with candles on every table. The aroma of fresh garlic permeating the air fills the senses.

"I love this time of year," says Lizzy.

"Me too," says Cici.

"I like visiting Fernandina Beach for New Year's Eve. There is very little traffic, and it feels like I am on vacation from the bustling city of Jacksonville," says Elle.

Ciao, the chef, is a friend of my son. Tonight he will take special care of our group.

"Hello, my darling Sara. It is so wonderful to see you, Weston, and your friends tonight. I have a special menu planned since we are celebrating New Year's Eve," says Ciao. "Michael and Cynthia told me you were coming tonight," he adds with a smile.

Ciao takes our menus and returns to the kitchen. A few minutes later, he returns with a platter of stuffed mushrooms, bruschetta, and a variety of cheeses and garlic knots.

"This smells divine; I can't wait to try the mushrooms. Thank you so much, Ciao," I say.

"Mmm, this garlic roll is yummy," says Lizzy after she takes a bite of the bread.

"If you would allow me, I will prepare a special dinner for you and your guests," says Ciao.

Everyone at the table shakes their heads in agreement. "It would be our pleasure to have you cook for us," I say.

The evening is filled with wine, excellent food, and fellowship.

"I can't remember when I have ever had such an incredible meal," says Ryan.

"Ciao, this was an amazing dinner. I can't thank you enough," I say.

"I am so full; I don't think I have ever eaten so much," says Weston.

"It has been my pleasure. My heart sings when I see my friends enjoying their meal," says Ciao.

"Thank you," says Elle.

"Thank you," says Lizzy.

"Here, here," says Cici.

"The food was fantastic," says Mary Beth.

Weston and Ryan split the bill, and we all decide to take a stroll down Centre Street toward the marina.

"This is one of the prettiest small towns during the holidays," says Mary Beth.

"Look, the yachts at the marina are lit up; the town is getting ready to drop the shrimp!" yells Cici grabbing my arm and rushing me toward the marina.

"But it is only eight o'clock!" I say.

"You know small towns; they drop the shrimp early so the children can enjoy New Year's Eve too!" Lizzy yells as we all run to the marina.

We arrive just as the lights on the shrimp light up.

"Ten, nine, eight, seven, six, five, four, three, two, one!" everyone yells. The ten-foot, pink-colored crystal shrimp drops from a thirty-foot pole. "Happy New Year!" we all yell. The little kids are waving small pink flags with tiny shrimp on each. Everyone is having a great time.

Standing behind me, Weston turns me to face him and gives me a New Year's kiss.

"Happy New Year, baby," he whispers into my ear, even though it is a bit early.

In Fernandina, it is New Year's Day.

Chapter Twenty-Four

The following Tuesday evening, I made a group call with Mary Beth and Lizzy.

"Hey, you are not going to believe what happened while I was in Biloxi. I wanted to tell you on New Year's Eve, but the others were there," I say.

"Did you win a bunch of money?" asks Mary Beth. "Did you meet Kevin Costner?" she adds.

"Did you win a car?" asks Lizzy.

"I did win some money, no car, but I found out who our murder victim is, and no, I did not meet Kevin Costner," I say.

"What!?" asks Lizzy.

"No," says Mary Beth. "I spoke with Snoop Dog last night, and she said the cops still didn't know his name."

"Well, I won a jackpot on the slot machine I was playing. The managers came over to take my picture for their Winner's Circle. Later, I walked over to where they hang the pictures of the winners, and there he was in a four feet by six feet picture frame hanging on the wall. I thought I was going to faint," I say.

"Who is he?" asks Lizzy.

"His name is Sonny Manuzco, and he lived in New York," I say. "Mary Beth, don't say anything to Snoop Dog. I have other plans, which I will share with all of you at dinner Thursday night," I add.

"Did you find out anything else about the guy?" Lizzy says eagerly.

"No," I reply.

What I didn't tell her was that Weston had noticed the silver pinky ring on the man's finger and remembered that he had seen it before at some union event. The day before the Beach Girl's dinner, Weston remembers about the ring.

"I know where I saw the pinky ring. It was at the union conference in Las Vegas. Some of the big union guys had them on. The local unions in New York and New Jersey give them to their union officers when the person has their twentieth anniversary. Your guy must have worked with one of those unions. I believe it will be one of the construction unions. I will check it out for you with some of the other business agents and see what else I can find out."

I pick up the house landline and call Mary Beth to tell her I can't make it to dinner the next night. I lie and tell her that I am sick with a cold.

How about I wait until February to tell the girls? I can get Mary Beth to check her friends at the postal service to see if Sonny has or had an address. And, maybe the DNA results will be back sooner than March or April, I think.

I call Mary Beth on Saturday and tell her the truth. "Mary Beth, the real reason I didn't come to the dinner is that I need you to see if you can get an address for Sonny Manuzco before I say anything else to the other girls. Also, Weston has identified the pinky ring, a construction union anniversary gift for their employees," I say.

"I knew you weren't sick. I know when you are hiding something," Mary Beth says. "Ok, I will see what I can do. I think I know someone who transferred from New York a few months ago. I'll let you know. Bye," she adds and hangs up the phone.

We wait until our February dinner before I say anything else about the case. The Beach Girls meet for dinner at River City Market Place on Thursday night. We have dinner at the Green Papaya restaurant. It has the best Thai food, and the atmosphere is very nice; it even has an indoor waterfall with soothing, flowing water.

I am really excited tonight; I have been thinking about this trip. I have plans for the girls and can hardly wait to tell them about the trip. The waiter comes over, and we place our drink orders. Since we are all back to work, we all order iced water or sweet "assed tay," which in regular English means sweet iced tea. Cici has a way with words, and they never get old.

"Hey girls, I have an update on our Sea Glass House case," I say. "When I was in Biloxi, I saw a picture of the murder victim at the Beaurivage Casino. Apparently, the man had won ten thousand dollars, and the casino administrators took his picture along with his big check. The date on the check said 2019. I was shocked and nearly fainted right there on the floor. His name is Sonny Manuzco, and he lived in New York City," I continue.

"Really?" asks Cici raising her eyes above her glasses to look at me.

"You have got to be kidding me," says Elle. "The results of the DNA came back yesterday; without a doubt, he has Italian roots. It appears his father was from northern Italy, and his mother was from Wales. That is an interesting combination," she adds.

"That makes sense; his name is Manuzco," I say.

"Besides finding out about Sonny, I won a good sum of money. I hit the jackpot on the "Shake the Apple Tree" slot machine, and the machine started going wild. Bright lights flashed on and off and a loud siren started blaring. I was shaking the devil out of that apple tree. I saw a few apples falling, and then a big golden apple fell out of the tree. People were standing around; Weston walked up and asked me what was happening. Then, the managers came up and told me I had won fifty thousand dollars. I was dancing and screaming; I got so excited that I almost peed in my pants. Of course, when Weston and I walked to the cashier's window, the IRS guy was waiting for us. It is amazing how much they want, but I did get enough to take us all for a three-day weekend in New York!" I exclaimed.

"Really? You are taking us to New York?" asks Mary Beth hugging my neck.

"Yes. I am paying for flights, rooms, food, and Broadway shows. We need to pick a weekend, Friday, Saturday, and Sunday. Mary Beth and I will leave on a Tuesday as I have a couple of things to do in New York. I would like you ladies to leave on Thursday no later than one o'clock if you all can plan on that. I will let Nancy know the plans so she can spend those days and nights with us. I will send you ladies the flight tickets. Mary Beth and I will meet you at the airport. By the way, bring some night-out clothes with you," I say. "Oh, and some warm clothes too. It is really cold there," I add.

"Oh my gawd," says Cici. "I am going to New York. You know it was on my bucket list," she says.

"Well, now you can scratch it off," I say.

"New York, New York," the girls begin to sing. "If I can make it there, I'll make it anywhere," they start singing.

"Pull out your phone calendar, Mary Beth, and let's set a date," I say.

"Let's go March eleventh through March fourteenth," says Elle.

"Ok. Everyone take those days off of work. I will get the plane tickets and the rooms," I say. "What Broadway shows do y'all want to see while we are there?" I ask.

"Let's go see Hamilton," says Lizzy. "I heard it was great. My sister went to see it when it was here at the Civic Tower in Jacksonville. She even bought the soundtrack and listens to it all the time," she adds.

"What about the Jersey Boys?" asks Mary Beth. "I love the music to that soundtrack. I chair dance to it as I drive."

"Ok, ladies; I will go ahead and get tickets to both the shows for all of us. Thank you, Jesus," I say, looking up to heaven and raising my hands.

"Amen," the others say.

Chapter Twenty-Five

The next day, I call Mary Beth. "Hey girl, I didn't want to say anything in front of the others last night, but I want us to go to New York early to check out Manuzco's house and where he works. Weston discovered that Manuzco worked for a local construction union in New York. And, you know, I am not great at getting flight tickets and rooms. Would you mind getting everything arranged? Let's get first-class tickets."

"Ok, where do you want to stay?" she asks.

"Make it someplace nice on Broadway, maybe the Plaza. We may never get to do this again; I want us to have fun and be treated like queens," I say. "I will take care of the show tickets and the limo service so we can pick the girls up from the airport when they arrive. Let me know which hotel, and I will call them with my credit card to reserve the rooms," I add.

I hang up and call Nancy, "Hey, girl. What are you doing?" I ask nonchalantly.

"Nothing much, just holding my sweet granddaughter," she says.

"Well, I won a bunch of money, fifty thousand at the casino, and I am giving all the Beach Girls a free trip to New York. I want you to take off and join us. I am paying for everything, including room, food, and Broadway shows. You just have to join us," I say with excitement.

"What?!" she yells, and I hear a little whimper coming from the baby.

"Yes, you heard right. We are coming up there on the afternoon of March 11th. We will return on the evening of March 14th. Mary Beth is setting up flights for us and reserving us rooms at a nice hotel on Broadway so we can be within a short driving distance of the shows. The girls picked the plays Hamilton and Jersey Boys; I hope you like those, too," I say.

"Yes, yes, yes!" Nancy says. "I am so excited and can't wait to see all the girls."

"We are just as excited," I say. "You keep snuggling with your granddaughter, and we will be in contact soon. Go ahead and apply for those days off," I say and hang up the phone.

The next couple of weeks, I attend my grandsons' football games. Rylan plays for his middle school team and is a running back and defensive player. Brooks plays for his high school team as a linebacker on defense and blocker on the putting and kickoff teams. I love to watch them run and tackle. They are both very good athletes in baseball and football, and Nana is so proud of them. All my grandchildren attend private schools and do very well academically.

When I attend their games, their sister, Caroline, brings her books to read to me in the stands or gets me to help her with her homework. She is in the third grade and is a little genius. Just the other day, her mother told me that she was speaking with the children about future jobs and that they should choose a job they would like to do but one that would help them make money. So that when they quit working, they can travel and do other things. Caroline speaks up and states, "I thought that was unemployment."

"Out of the mouths of babes," it is said. My family has been very blessed, and we have worked very hard for the things we have.

I laugh and shake my head. "She has a point in today's world," I say. We were at an equestrian show with Caroline that day, and she won a third-place ribbon. This was her first competition; she really wanted to win first prize. After her ride, she looked sad. When I asked, "What's the matter, baby?"

"I only won third place; I wanted to win first," she whimpered.

"Well, look at it this way. This is your first competition, and the ribbon is pink. It is the prettiest ribbon out here," I said.

"Oh Nana, even though it is not first place, it is the prettiest ribbon," she said, holding it proudly as I took a picture.

All the Beach Girls have grandchildren, and we know that in today's culture, spending time with the kids is difficult as they are so busy. When I was young, I spent a lot of time on my grandfather's farm and played with my cousins. Today's kids have tons of activities; grandmas just try to stay flexible and do what they can.

On the first Saturday of March, Mary Beth gives me a call. "Hey, I got us two first-class tickets to New York on March 9th. I got the others first-class tickets for March 11th; they should arrive in New York around four in the afternoon. I found the Crown Plaza on Broadway and reserved three rooms each having two queen beds. We are right down there where the action will be. Especially, after the Beach Girls arrive in town. Give the Plaza a call with your credit card number," she giggles. "They are waiting for your call," she adds.

"Thanks, Mary Beth," I say. "I have ordered and paid for our show tickets. They will be at the will-call windows at each theatre for the shows. Friday night, we will be going to the Barrymore Theatre to see Hamilton, and on Saturday night, we will go to the Broadway Theatre to see the Jersey Boys. I have also made reservations for dinner after Saturday's show at Carmine's Italian restaurant. I hear it is the best Italian restaurant in New York City. Of course, we will have to be there thirty minutes before the show begins, but they both will have bars open when we pick up the tickets," I say.

"That sounds wonderful. I am getting so excited; can we leave today?" she asks.

"I have also contacted a limo service and arranged for the service to pick us up an hour before the other girls arrive in New York so we can be there waiting for them. Cici might get the girls lost in that big airport. Remember the time Cici drove herself to the beach house in St. Augustine and went to the wrong house? I wish I could have seen the look on those people's faces when Cici walked right into their house," I say.

"Yes, that was funny. She thought she was at the right house because she couldn't read the addresses," says Mary Beth.

"You and I will take a taxi to the hotel on Tuesday when we get into New York," I say.

"Will we rent a car for Wednesday?" Mary Beth asks.

"Yes, the rental company will have one outside the Crown Plaza at nine o'clock Wednesday morning," I respond. "We will drop it off in front of the Plaza and call them to pick it up when we are through using the car," I add.

"That's good. I have a friend who used to work for the New York branch of the postal service. I asked him if he knew about the location of the address. Apparently, it is in a small neighborhood on the outskirts of Little Italy in New York City. My friend is going to draw me a map of the

Plaza just in case we get lost. We can put the address into the navigation unit in the rental car, too," Mary Beth says.

"Make sure you don't mention this to the other girls. I don't want anyone to get hurt or upset if things go wrong. It is bad enough that you and I are doing this crazy thing," I say.

"Don't worry, I have a concealed weapon permit," says Mary Beth.

"Mary Beth, you can't take the gun with us on the plane. We could be arrested at the airport," I say.

"Oh yeah, I forgot my certificate is only for Florida," she sighs.

"We will buy a stun gun when we get to New York, just for precaution," I say.

"How big can we get? Are you buying?" she asks.

"I am going to get the biggest one that will fit in my purse," I say.

"Your purse is the size of a cell phone," she says.

"You get yours, and I'll get mine. I am not planning on hurting anyone," I say.

Chapter Twenty-Six

On the morning of the trip, Weston and I pick Mary Beth up from her house and drive to the Jacksonville airport. Weston pulls up to the departure entrance and stops the car.

"You two are not doing anything stupid, are you?" he asks, knowing full well that he would rather not know.

"No, baby, it is just a fun weekend for us girls. We have two Broadway shows and a little shopping to do. That's all," I say, partially truthful. "Can I pick up something for you in New York?" I ask.

Mary Beth says, "Weston, you know us. We never get into trouble."

"All I need is for you girls to be safe and to have fun," replies Weston.

Weston gets our luggage from the back of the SUV and takes it up to the baggage loading area outside the airport. He kisses me goodbye and shakes his head at Mary Beth. We both laugh.

We make our way to the security area and get in a line that must be two football field lengths long. We have our masks on and wear our slip-on sandals so that when we get our turn to enter the metal detectors, we can slip off our shoes and place them in the basket with our purses. Mary Beth goes through the security check first, and the alarm goes off. For a moment, I wonder if she has brought her gun. She backs out to go through the security check again and stops. She tells the security officer, "I forgot, I have ten pins and screws in my right ankle. It is from a four-wheeler accident." Mary Beth has to go to another line to be checked out with the wand; she makes it through.

"Whew," I said. I went straight through without any problem. Mary Beth is behind me. We hit the nearest café for coffee and Danish, realizing we still had an hour before our flight would board. After two cups of black coffee, we head to the boarding site. Since we are flying first class, we board first. I get the window seat, and Mary Beth sits on the aisle. A good-looking man sits next to Mary Beth, and I can feel her excitement. For me, it is a good time to take a nap, so I turn toward the window and doze off before the takeoff.

"Wake up, wake up, we are landing in a few minutes," Mary Beth says, shaking my arm

"Ok, I am awake. Do you have any water?" I ask.

"No, but I can get the stewardess to bring us some," Mary Beth replies.

Mary Beth signals the stewardess and asks for two bottles of spring water. My throat is dry. Lord, I hope I didn't snore. "Mary Beth, did I snore?" I whisper.

"No, you were sound asleep. I did meet the gentleman in the next seat, though. He was a New Yorker and asked where we were staying. He said he might meet up with us sometime this weekend," says Mary Beth.

"I wouldn't bet on it. We are going to be pretty busy," I say.

Mary Beth turns and smiles at the gentleman. I notice he was staring at her boobs.

"Mary Beth, look at where his eyes are staring. I don't know what I am going to do with you," I add, shaking my head.

Our plane arrives at the airport on time. As soon as the door opens, Mary Beth and I make a beeline to the exit. I need to use the bathroom before we pick up our luggage.

"Mary Beth, I have to pee; move faster," I say.

"Ok... ok. I am going as fast as I can with these sandals on. They don't want to stay on my feet," she says, waddling like a duck.

"Could it be because they are two sizes too big for your feet?" I exclaim

"I like my slippers big and comfy," yells Mary Beth trying to keep up with me.

We finally make it to the bathroom, and I am so happy. Those two cups of coffee are screaming to get out of my bladder. We make our way to the luggage pickup turnstile and grab our suitcases. I see a man with a luggage carrier and hire him and a porter to take our things to the taxi pickup area. I hand the porter a twenty to split with his helper and thank the young men for their service. Mary Beth sees the man from the plane and slyly waves to him; she doesn't notice the woman in the car picking him up.

"Mary Beth, stop waving; there is a woman in the car," I say.

"Oh no!" she exclaims. "That turd. I thought he was a nice guy."

We grab a taxi and arrive at the Crown Plaza thirty minutes later. New York City was abuzz at three o'clock in the afternoon, and people were everywhere. The streets were lined up with delivery trucks honking and people crowding intersections waiting for the traffic lights to signal them to walk. It was so crowded that the people looked more like colors morphing together than actual people. Our taxi driver almost hit a woman wearing black leather pants and a black jacket as she walks her stylish gray poodle. She didn't see us coming and walked out into the intersection; she never bothered to look. Luckily the taxi driver saw her and stopped. He yells out the taxi window, "Hey, lady, watch where you are going." She growls at him like a dog and keeps on walking. You have to love this town and its people.

After the taxi driver drops us off in front of the hotel and the porters at the Crown Plaza gather our luggage, we register at the desk for our room.

"Thank you, ladies for joining us this week. I hope you enjoy your stay, and if you need anything, just dial five for your concierge, Mathew," the gentleman at registration says to Mary Beth and me.

We grab our key cards and head to the elevator. Mary Beth pushes the seventh-floor button, and the elevator begins to move. Mathew, an attractive twenty-something-year-old man, meets us at the elevator doors and ushers us to our room.

"We have cocktails and hors d'oeuvres at four o'clock in the seventh floor dining area. I look forward to seeing you ladies," says Mathew, smiling.

Our room is a suite with two bedrooms, each with a queen bed and balcony overlooking Broadway. There are fresh white calla lilies and white hydrangeas in large vases in both the living area and the bedrooms. The fragrances of the flowers in the room make me feel like I am in a beautiful garden.

"Mary Beth, this room and the view from the balcony are breathtaking," I say.

I walk out on the balcony and sit down on the floral sofa admiring the scenery. I can see both of the theatres from here. It will take no time for us girls to get to the shows. Mary Beth joins me on the balcony and sits down, stretching her short legs.

"Thank you so much for this trip. You know you didn't have to do this; we would have all paid to come," said Mary Beth.

"I know I didn't have to do it; I just wanted to share my gift with all the Beach Girls, I said.

After fifteen minutes, I say, "It's four o'clock. Let's go over to the dining area for a drink."

"Sure, let me check my hair and makeup first. I might see someone I would like to meet," says Mary Beth with a twinkle in her blue eyes.

"Ok, but I am not dragging you away this time," I say, laughing.

We walk to the dining area and can't believe our eyes. In the middle of the dining room is an enormous buffet table with beautifully prepared delights. Luckily for us, there are only two other people in the room, along with Mathew, so we don't have to be secretive about the amount of food we eat. Yes, we know how to behave in public, but when no one is looking, who cares how much food is on our plate. I walk up to the buffet table, pick up a Crown Plaza china plate, and begin selecting chilled boiled shrimp, meatballs wrapped in bacon dipped in a spicy sauce, tiny Brussel sprouts toasted in a brown sugar and honey sauce. I pick up a soft, wheat, hard roll with a couple of slices of brie. I place the plate on our table and return to the buffet. I grab a bowl and fill it with fresh pineapple chunks, blueberries, and a petite slice of watermelon. I wonder where the fruit comes from this time of year since it is not a native food to New Yorkers.

Mary Beth returns to our table with a plate piled high with shrimp, cabbage-wrapped spring rolls, meatballs, and a couple of hard rolls. Her metabolism is very unique. She can eat whatever she wants and never gains a pound. She goes back to the buffet table, picks up another plate, and adds a couple of pastries, cheese and apple, and chocolate cookies to her plate.

"Can you believe this buffet?" she says.

"I know, it's great; we won't need dinner tonight," I say. "After eating, let's go to Sak's 5th Avenue to do some shopping. I need to buy a black dress for an upcoming event Weston and I are attending at the college. The Gold Key recipients at the University of North Florida are having a gala to celebrate the school's 50th anniversary."

"Also, we need to get a couple of stun guns," adds Mary Beth. "I have a few bucks saved up, and a cute little dress is on my list."

We finish our meal, which was delicious, and go back to the room for our purses. We head to the elevator, where Mathew is waiting for us.

"Did you ladies say you wanted to go to Sak's 5th Avenue?" he asks.

"Yes, we did," I say.

"I will have a car waiting for you downstairs," he replied.

"Thank you so kindly, Mathew," Mary Beth states in her best southern drawl.

We get into the elevator and push the button for the lobby.

"I don't think I have ever been treated like a princess before," says Mary Beth.

"Well, enjoy it while you can," I say. "It may be a while before your prince charming comes along," I add.

"Yes, I usually get stuck with the frog," quips Mary Beth.

We walk outside the hotel, and a car immediately pulls up.

"Ladies, do you want to go to Sak's 5th Avenue?" the driver, wearing a New York cap, asks.

"Yes, thank you," we both say at the same time.

We arrive at Sak's, and the driver opens the doors for us.

"Here is my card. Please call me when you are ready to leave, and I will be right here for you," he says.

I tip him a twenty and head to a shop with Mary Beth. We enter a women's boutique and search the racks for a black cocktail dress. I don't see anything I like for the warm weather in Florida, so I look for some leather pants. The weather is cold here, and leather keeps a person warm. I try on several and select a pair of black leather jeans made by Jexi Howard. She is the newest designer for Sak's. After purchasing my size eight, black, tight jeans for three hundred and seventy dollars and a red, silk, low-cut blouse for two hundred and sixty dollars, I begin looking for Mary Beth. I find her in the petite section, trying on red leather dress pants with black stripes. She is a Georgia Bulldog, and anything black and red she tries on and usually buys. She walks out of the dressing area wearing red and black pants and a beautiful black cowl neck sweater; she looks adorable.

"Get those; they look amazing on you," I state. "We need to look for the stun guns when you are ready."

Mary Beth purchases the pants and sweater, and we head down the escalator to the exit. We exit through the front doors and walk a block down the street. We pass by a small storefront, and I immediately stop.

"Hey, they sell stun guns inside the store we just passed," I tell Mary Beth.

"Let's go get one," she responds.

We turn around and walk inside up to the counter. "I would like a small stun gun," I say.

"We have a section over here in the cabinet," the salesman advises as he walks us down the aisle.

I look into the glass cabinet and select a Sabre 1,820 UC green stun gun. Mary Beth selects a Taser X2 Professional Series 22, the big daddy of Tasers. I purchase the batteries and the guns, and we leave the store.

"Mary Beth, put your stun gun away. Someone is going to knock you in the head and steal it," I whisper to her.

"Alright. I am not scared, are you?" she says.

"No, I'm tired," I say.

"Me, too," says Mary Beth. "Let's call the driver."

I call the driver, and he immediately picks up.

"Yes, ma'am," he says. "Are you ladies ready to be chauffeured to the Crown Plaza?" he asks.

"Yes, we have shopped until we are dropping," I say.

"I am waiting right outside, miss," he says.

"Thank you," I say, and we hurry back to Macy's and see our driver next to the awaiting car."

The driver opens the doors, and we flop into the back seat. He drops us off at the entrance to our hotel, and we immediately head up to our room. Mathew is waiting at the elevator.

"How was your shopping trip?" he asks.

"Great," we both say in unison, holding up our shopping bags.

Once inside our room, we unpack our luggage and settle in for the night. Mary Beth and I load the batteries into our protective weapons and return to our bedrooms. I place my gun into a small pocket in my purse. If I know Mary Beth, she has hers on the nightstand. I shower and head to bed; tomorrow will be a very busy day. We will both need our rest tonight.

Chapter Twenty-Seven

We awake around seven thirty and make coffee in our room It is a little chilly this morning, so we grab blankets and head to the balcony to watch New Yorkers scurry along the sidewalks to work. A cab driver pokes his head out of the driver's side window to yell to a man crossing the street to "get the hell out of the way!" I laugh as the walker shakes his fist back at the taxi driver. I think, *road rage is everywhere.*

We finally get dressed, stop by the dining area, pick up a Danish and a cup of coffee each, and head to the elevator. Mathew is there waiting.

"Good morning, ladies. Off to see the sights?" he asks.

"Yes, we have a rental car for today and want to visit a friend outside the city. Have a great day!" I say, and Mary Beth pushes the lobby button in the elevator.

Our car is waiting for us right outside the Crown Plaza. It is a small, white Chevy SUV, Equinox. The interior is grey with black leather and all the electrical devices a person could want. I slide into the seat, move it closer to the steering wheel, and start the engine. The heater is already on, and the heated seats are nice and cozy.

Mary Beth sets the navigator for Manuzco's house address as I drive away from the hotel. Driving through New York City is like being a hamster going through a maze. Turn right, turn left, turn right again, and you are in the tunnel. We reach the area for Manuzco's house but can't find the street. A couple blocks down the road, Mary Beth sees a mail carrier truck.

"Pull up next to the mail carrier. I'll ask him how to find the address," she says.

I pull up next to the truck, Mary Beth pushes a button, and the passenger side car window begins to move down,

"Hello, sir," she says in her southern drawl. "Can you please help me?" she asks.

"Sure, what can I do for you, lady?" the mail carrier asks.

"Well, I am looking for this address, and we can't find the road. I work for the postal service in Jacksonville, Florida. Perhaps you know my friend Jerry Sigmund; he used to work in New York?" she says, smiling.

"Are you talking about Gerald Sigmund, who worked in the sorting department?" the mail carrier asks.

"Yes, Gerald, we call him Jerry," she says.

"Yes, Gerald is a good friend. Tell him Jimmy Seroni says hello. What was that address you ladies were looking for?" he asks.

"It is 144 Cross Sabatini Way," Mary Beth says.

"Ok, turn around and turn at the first left. It is hard to see because of the trees, but right next to the road is a red brick house with brown shutters. That address is the third house on the right. Now, don't forget to tell Gerald his old friend Jimmy asked about him," he says.

"Thanks, and I will, Jimmy," Mary Beth responds.

"Cool move," I say and head back the way we came. I drive past Manuzco's house to the end of his road. There are ten houses, all red brick with brown trim. The neighborhood looks nice; there are only a couple of cars parked on the street. I pull into Manuzco's driveway, and Mary Beth and I walk to the front door. I knock on the door; an elderly woman opens it. Mary Beth has moved near the side of the house, and when the lady answers the door, she slips quickly around the house.

"Can I help you?" she asks. She is wearing a simple, green, floral house dress with closed-in brown shoes that slide on her feet. The elderly looks to be about eighty years old. She has curly, gray hair cut just above her shoulders. She must be Sonny's mother.

"I am looking for Sonny Manuzco; this is the address I have for him," I say.

"I am Sonny's mother. I haven't heard from him since he went to Florida," she says. "Who are you?" she adds.

"I am from the Department of Transportation and would like to speak with Sonny concerning some equipment he rented from my client. Do you know any way I can reach him?" I ask, pretending to be a worker from the DOT.

"Well, he works for the Concrete and Cement Local 23 on Baywood Street. I have called them several times, and they say he is still in Florida. If you find him, tell him to call his mother. I am really worried about Sonny," she says.

"Thank you, and have a blessed day," I say and turn toward the car. The lady goes inside her house and closes the door. I walk back to the Equinox and open the door. I look back at the house and see no sign of Mary Beth. I start the car, put it in reverse, and back out into the road.

While I was talking with Manuzco's mother, Mary Beth went wandering around outside of the house. As I look out the review mirror, Mary Beth suddenly appears, walking back onto the sidewalk. She continues past a couple of the brick houses on the block, and that's when I pull up next to her. Mary Beth gets into the car and buckles her seat belt. I push the gas pedal down and ease our way out of the neighborhood.

"There is a brand new Cadillac SUV in the garage, and it appears they are the only ones on the block with a satellite dish in the backyard. It is not the kind of satellite that connects to the television. It looks like one of those international satellites I have seen before at the main post office in Jacksonville. That satellite connects to other countries. I took a photo of it and sent the picture to my friend, William. He is the techie for the postal service. He will know the purpose this satellite is used for. The dish for the TV is located on the top of the roof like other neighbors," states Mary Beth

"Great job, Mary Beth. I knew I brought you along for something," I say with a smile. "Proud of you, girl," I add, giving her a high five.

Before heading back to the city, we stop at an Italian family restaurant for lunch. We want to try some authentic Italian cuisine. I park the car in the parking lot of a strip mall, and we walk into the quaint Italian family restaurant. The place is very dark with muted light and has red leather booths on each side of the windows looking out at the parking lot. A small bar is at the back of the restaurant, and small, round tables for four diners are scattered throughout. The aromas originating out of the kitchen are heavenly; yummy garlic smells permeate the dining room, making my stomach growl. A sign displaying "seat yourself" hangs from the hostess table. Mary Beth and I select a table in the middle near the restroom. A young Italian girl brings us menus and takes our drink order; I order a diet Coke with ice and Mary Beth selects sweet tea. Of course, not being in the south, sugar does not come with the tea. Once we get our drinks, we order our lunch. I order their homemade lasagna and an Italian salad with olives. Mary Beth orders chicken parmesan and a

Caesar salad. The young waitress, Maria, goes into the kitchen to take our orders and comes back with the most mouthwatering garlic knots.

"Would you like some olive oil and vinaigrette with your bread?" she asks.

"That would be lovely," says Mary Beth.

She brings the dipping sauce, and I ask, "Do you know a guy by the name of Sonny Manuzco?"

"Yea, I know, Sonny. I grew up in this neighborhood, and he was always around giving us kids a hard time. Why? Did something happen to him?" she asks.

"No, no, we were just at his mother's house. She said he went to Florida and hasn't heard from him since. Have you seen him around?" I ask.

"The last time I saw him, he and Rudy Caruso were having dinner and talking about a cement drop in Florida. He works in the concrete business," says Maria.

"Check up!" the cook in the kitchen yells.

"That's your food," the waitress says. Thank goodness she left the table because Mary Beth's eyes were staring at me. She has that deer-in-the-headlights look.

"It's ok, Mary Beth, calm down," I say.

Maria brings us our food with steam coming from the hot plates. The lasagna is the best I have ever eaten; stringy cheese and full of fresh garlic. The salad is fresh, as if they had just pulled the lettuce out of the garden. I know Mary Beth is enjoying hers as she moans the whole way through the meal.

"This is amazing," I said.

"Mmm," moans Mary Beth, placing another forkful into her mouth.

Maria comes by to drop off our checks, and I ask, "Do you know where Concrete and Cement Local 23 is around here?"

"Yes, go two blocks down the road out front and turn right. You can't miss it; it is a large red, two stories brick building with white columns in front. The parking lot is in the back of the building." Maria says.

Mary Beth and I get into the Equinox and buckle the seatbelts. I put the car in drive and turn out of the lot. We drive the two blocks and turn right onto Piedmont Avenue. About a tenth of a mile, I see the big Local 23 building. Maria was right; the place must have ten Grecian columns in the front of the building. We park in the back parking lot.

"Mary Beth, we are just going in and looking around to see if we find any pictures of Sonny. Let me do the talking, I say."

"Ok," she says.

As we walk in, a pretty Italian female receptionist welcomes us, "Hello ladies, can I help you?"

"We are just visiting a friend in New York, and while we were driving around, I noticed your local. My husband is the business agent for a Tampa, Florida, union, Local 16, and I thought I would drop by and see your building," I say with a smile on my face.

"Come on; I'll show you around. We are very proud of our building. Our Local has been around since nineteen fifty-one. Here is our conference room, and the pictures on the wall are all the officers our board has had over the past seventy years," she says.

"Look, Mary Beth, the suits the men have worn over the years are wonderful. In this one, the jackets are long and the sleeves are shorter than the shirt sleeves. The recent officers are very distinguished looking. One of the guys in this picture is wearing a zoot suit. They are all very handsome men," I say, looking for a picture of Sonny.

The pretty receptionist shows us around for a while. Heading back, we thank her for the hospitality. We get in the SUV, and Mary Beth says, "I saw Sonny, and I noticed that all of them wear the same kind of pinkie ring."

"I saw that too," I say, raising my eyebrows.

"When the girls get here tomorrow, we will fill them in on everything we have found out and decide our next move," says Mary Beth.

"I don't want to talk about that while we are in New York. Let's forget all of this and just have a good time with the girls," I say.

"Ok, it will be more fun if we don't discuss what we know," says Mary Beth.

Chapter Twenty-Eight

We drive back to the Crown Plaza Hotel and leave the car out front with the valet. I call the rental company to send someone to pick up the SUV. We get into our elevator and push the button for the seventh floor. Mathew is waiting for us.

"Good afternoon, ladies. Have you been enjoying your day?" he asks.

"Yes, Mathew, we have. Now we are ready for a massage. Would it be possible for you to set that up for us, please?" I ask.

"Of course; would you like that massage in your room?" he asks.

"Yes, that would be nice. We would both like massages," I said.

"I will arrange for your massages, say at three o'clock?" Mathew asks.

"Three o'clock will be very nice," I say.

Mary Beth and I head to the room to put on our comfortable clothes. Wearing heels and a pants suit all day is not our normal attire.

Investigating has its issues, and dressing for the role of a businesswoman can be stressful. I can hear the cotton nightie and slippers calling my name.

We quickly change our clothes, and at three o'clock, the massage therapists, as they inform us of their titles at the onset, come into the room and take us to our separate bedrooms for the massages. The therapist sets up her table and plays some relaxing ocean wave sounds as she prepares her lotions. She leaves the room and lets me change into the sheet she has left behind. When the therapist returns, she pours warm oil over my back and rubs my neck and lower back, releasing the tightness in the muscles. After a few minutes, I drift off to sleep. After an hour of massaging and sleeping, the therapist wakes me up.

"Wow... that was amazing. I have never gone to sleep during a massage," I say.

"You were very tense when I first started. I finished up about fifteen minutes ago and let you sleep while I cleaned up my things," she says.

She walks out of the room while I get dressed. I open the door to let her know she can come in and finish getting her things. I opened my purse and pulled out two fifties.

"Please give one to the other therapist. Thank you so much," I say.

Mary Beth was already dressed and on the balcony. She has a glass of wine in her hand, watching the people and traffic scurrying about.

"Hey girl, you finally up? I heard you fell asleep," she says. "You won't believe what I just saw down there. You know that guitar-playing cowboy who wears very little clothes?" she asks.

"Yes, I have seen him on TV before," I say.

"Well, he was standing in front of the theatre across the street. I took a picture; see?" asks Mary Beth.

"He only has on cowboy boots and bikini underwear!" I squeal, laughing and dancing around. "He has to be freezing. Leave it to you to see something like that in New York," I add.

"What do you want to do this evening? The Metropolitan Museum of Art has a Roman pottery showing tonight at eight o'clock, or we could go to the Museum of Modern Art," I said.

"Let's have a snack and a drink here at the Palm Court and then go to the Museum of Modern Art," says Mary Beth. "I saw enough Roman pottery when I was in Italy to last me a lifetime," she adds as she gets up and goes inside her room. Mary Beth is a world traveler and has visited a lot of countries.

We dress in wool slacks with colorful sweaters and comfortable walking boots. The museum is nearby, so we decide to walk there after dinner at the Palm Garden restaurant in the Plaza.

We grab our purses and coats and take the elevator down to the lobby. We walk across the lobby toward the Palm Garden restaurant. The waiter brings water and fresh rolls. A waitress comes over and asks, "Would you ladies like a drink from our bar" she asks.

"Yes, would you please bring us a carafe of your Moscato wine, please," I say.

"Of course," she says.

She heads over to the bar and brings back a bottle of Moscato, removes the cork, and pours us both a small portion. I swirl the wine around in my glass, taking in the aroma.

"Delicious, thank you very much," I say.

"Will you ladies be dining with us tonight?" she says.

"Yes, I would like a small cup of clam chowder," says Mary Beth.

"And I will have the small Caesar salad," I say.

The waitress delivers our orders to the chef and moves to another table. Mary Beth leans back in her chair and says, "Sara, this has been a remarkable day. First, we investigated Sonny's world. Then, we have an incredible lunch in Little Italy. When we got back, we had a fantastic massage, and now we are eating at the Palm Garden in the Plaza on Times Square."

"Look over at the food coming out of the kitchen; that plate of food is beautiful," I say as the waiter places the steak pie in front of the gentleman at the table next to us. The steak pie is sculpted with pastry leaves of brown and orange colors, like a fall picture.

"The chef is an artist," I say.

"Wait until you taste it," Mary Beth says as she places her second spoonful of clam chowder into her mouth. She looks at me with a twinkle in her eye and begins to sing, "I'm in heaven, I'm in heaven, and I don't want to ever go home." We both laugh.

We finish our dinner with our bottle of Moscato, and I signal the waiter over.

"Please charge this to my room and give our wait staff this," I say, handing him two fifty-dollar bills. I know that a hefty tip is already included in the check. These people work really hard, and I appreciate them. After all, "This is fun money," says Weston.

"Thank you," he says, smiling, and off he goes.

We gather our coats off our chairs and head outside into a chilly evening. We walk along Broadway making our way among all the tourists and natives of New York. Everyone moves at a fast pace, and we jump right in with them. We arrive at the Museum of Modern Art and purchase tickets. Since we will be here a while, we decide to check our coats. Mary Beth and I walk over to the coat check counter and give our coats to the attendant. We receive our tickets.

Upon entry to the gallery, I spy a huge black painting on the second floor. It looks a little ridiculous, a solid black painting.

"I can do that," I say as we move up the winding staircase. It appears to be more three-dimensional. The closer we get to the art piece, it begins to look like a bunch of flies pasted onto a large, black canvas. Yes, that is what it is; a million flies on a black canvas. Why couldn't I think of that art? Well, because I am not crazy. It may be art to some, but to me, it was nasty.

We go further into the gallery, and Mary Beth whispers, "Come here. I want to show you something."

"What is it?" I say.

"Look at that painting with the naked people holding hands in a circle," she laughs. "They don't have any boy and girl parts. I think my grandkids can do a better job. At least they would put clothes on the people. Jackson would make sure the boys had wieners," she adds.

"Well, I think the artist is saying that men and women should be considered equal in today's culture and that by accepting this concept, we can exist in peace," I say.

"That sounds like an appropriate interpretation," says Mary Beth, and we laugh at ourselves.

The museum is beautiful; we really enjoy the "Flag" painting and "Campbell Soup Can Labels" print. Around ten, we decide to walk back to the hotel and stop at Starbucks along the way.

"I guess they are right; there is a Starbucks every two blocks in New York," I say.

I order a black coffee, and Mary Beth orders a latte with whipped cream. We sit near the front window and watch people pass by. "I don't think I could live here with all the people and noise from the sirens, cars, and cranes," I say.

"Me neither. I like the Florida beaches and warm weather. Look! It is Matthew Perkins, the guy from the movie about dinosaurs in Hawaii," says Mary Beth. "He is even better looking in person," she adds.

"Yea, he is a good-looking man," I say.

Mary Beth quickly gets out of her chair, grabs her camera, and heads out the door, following Mr. Perkins. I see through the window that she catches up to him and the two get a selfie with Mary Beth's camera. She returns to the table with a huge grin.

"Got it," she says.

I just shake my head and return to my coffee.

After a little people-watching, we go back to the Crown Plaza and catch the elevator to the seventh floor. Mathew was waiting for us.

"I wonder if he ever sleeps," I whisper to Mary Beth.

"Hello, Mathew," says Mary Beth. "It has been a fabulous day, and we are going to bed," she adds.

"Good night, ladies," says Mathew. "Will you need a wake-up call for in the morning?" he asks.

"No, thank you, Mathew," I say as I head to the room

Chapter Twenty-Nine

The next morning, we decide to wake up at nine o'clock. Wrapped up in blankets, we have coffee on the balcony and enjoy the Times Square view. This city never sleeps, and the excitement is exhilarating. Out on the sidewalk is a group of vacationers. They look up toward our balcony and wave. We wave back, and they take a few pictures.

"I guess they think we are somebody since we are staying at the Plaza," I say.

"What are we doing today?" asks Mary Beth after taking a sip of coffee.

"I don't know, what would you like to do?" I respond.

"Well, since the Beach Girls will get in around four o'clock, why don't we go to Chelsea for some shopping? We can look around for our dresses and have lunch at Westfield Chelsea. I heard the food is fresh and really good," says Mary Beth.

"Sounds good to me," I say.

We dress in boots, jeans, sweaters, and parkas. As I pick up my purse, the phone rings.

"Hello," I say not recognizing the number.

"Ms. Springs," she says.

"Yes."

"You don't know me, but I think you should know that there are people asking about you. Please be careful and watch your back," she hangs up.

"Oh my Lord," I say.

"Who was it?" asks Mary Beth.

"It was a woman telling me that people are asking about me and that I need to watch my back," I murmur.

"Did you recognize the voice?" asks Mary Beth.

"You know, now that I think about it, I think I do. It was the woman at the union hall. I did tell her where we were staying," I said.

"Do you have your stun gun in your purse?" asks Mary Beth.

"Yes. Do you?" I ask.

"Yes, you know I do. Ok, this is what we are going to do. We will get a cab to Chelsea and visit a few of the shops. Let's make sure we stay together and look around in case we are being followed," says Mary Beth.

"Ok, that sounds like a good plan. I will get reservations at Westfield Chelsea for twelve-thirty with a table facing the windows. That way, we will always be in full view and can keep an eye out if someone is looking for us. After lunch, we will get a cab back to the hotel, and then we can get ready to meet the girls at the airport. Even if someone follows us, they will not see anything important or questionable. Don't mention this to the other girls. We need to just keep a good watch and enjoy the weekend," I say.

Mathew meets us at the elevator, "Good morning, ladies. Got some big plans for today?"

"Just a little shopping and then our friends will arrive this afternoon. They are going to be so excited to be here," I say.

"I will call down for a car for you ladies, and here is a card for a driver to pick you up when you are ready to return to the Plaza," says Mathew.

"Thanks, Mathew," says Mary Beth giving him a little wink.

"Thanks, Mathew," I say.

As we walk outside the Plaza, the wind is barely blowing, and the weather is a little crisp. Our driver is waiting for us by the front door of the hotel.

"We would like to go to Chelsea for some shopping. Please drop us off where most New York visitors like to shop. Today is for mingling with the crowds," I say, smiling at the driver.

The cab driver lets us out in front of Banks and Co. clothing boutique. We slowly walk indoors, looking for others getting out of cabs along the block. We didn't see anyone else that didn't look like a tourist.

"I guess we are safe," I say to Mary Beth.

"Oh, look, Sara. This scarf would look great on you," she says, holding up a Picasso-style black scarf with the white outline of a naked man.

"I think you should get it," I say, and we both start giggling.

"Now this is really cute," Mary Beth says as she picks up a Wang Wang bag which is a small purse with a tiny hidden pocket. The preteens love them.

"It is very pretty; maybe I'll get it for Caroline. She likes the colorful, small purses to keep her money and small hairbrush in when we go shopping," I say.

"She will love it," says Mary Beth.

I purchase the purse; Mary Beth and I walk out the door, looking both ways for anything suspicious. I spot a burly Italian man a couple of stores behind us. He is talking on his cell phone. He quickly turns around, facing away from us.

"I think that man is following us," I say.

"I see him; don't look back. Just keep moving forward as if we don't notice him. He will be very sorry he followed us. Let's keep moving and see how long he lasts," laughs Mary Beth.

"Yeah, I don't think he can walk a half block, much less a half mile. He looks like he is wearing dress shoes," I reply, giving out a little snort.

We walk a few blocks glancing in the windows of the stores at the items and checking for a reflection of our follower. Apparently, the man can't keep up.

"Ok, here we are at the Westfield. Let's eat," I say.

"Yes, I am starving. After walking so much, my little tootsies are tired. I bet we have walked ten city blocks," she says.

"Even if we have been walking two miles a day at home, ten blocks is a long way. I bet our follower is passed out on the sidewalk in front of one of the stores," I say as we enter the restaurant.

"We have reservations at twelve-thirty; the name is Springs," I say.

"Please, this way Ms. Springs," the waitress states.

The beautiful waitress sits us next to the front windows where we have a clear view of the street.

"Ladies, may I start you off with a glass of wine?" she says.

"Yes, I would like a glass of white zinfandel, please," says Mary Beth.

"I will have the same, please," I say.

The waitress returns to the table with our wine and a small tray of cheese and toast tips.

"Thank you," I say.

"Thank you," says Mary Beth.

"Would you ladies like to order now?" she asks.

"Yes, I would like your Caesar salad with the grilled shrimp and bacon bites," I say, thinking that Cici would be proud of me.

"I will have the Caesar salad with grilled chicken," says Mary Beth.

While waiting for our order, Mary Beth and I savor our cheese and toast tips.

"This cheese is amazing; I think it is brie; the softness inside is so delicate," says Mary Beth.

"Do you see anything outside?" I ask, focusing on the crowd of people passing by the window.

"No, do you?" she asks me.

"No, I guess we lost him," I say.

"Let's enjoy our lunch and call a cab," she says, siping wine.

Our Caesar salads arrive, and we dive in. The lunch is superb; Mary Beth and I enjoy every minute of it. After lunch, I call for the car. We wait inside the restaurant until it arrives. We get into the black SUV and head back to the Plaza to prepare to meet the girls at the airport.

Walking into the Plaza, I hear, "Sara, Mary Beth!"

Chapter Thirty

I turn to look, and there is Nancy waving and hurrying over to us.

"Hey Nancy, I am so glad you made it. Where is your luggage? You are staying, aren't you?" I ask curiously.

"Yes, I am staying the weekend. My luggage has already been sent up to my room, and I have met Mathew. What a sweet man," she says.

We head up to our rooms stopping at Nancy and Cici's room first. It is set up just like mine, and the live flowers are breathtaking.

Nancy says, "Sara, this is so nice of you. I am so appreciative of your kindness." She hugs my neck. I can tell that she is very happy.

"The girls are flying in at four, and we are meeting the limo downstairs in a few minutes. I can't wait to get everyone here so we can party!" I squeal.

"Mary Beth, you look wonderful. Have you girls been behaving?" asks Nancy.

"Innocent until proven guilty," says Mary Beth.

"Did you have a difficult time getting away from work," I ask Nancy, who works for the Drug Enforcement Agency.

"No, I have plenty of days. They know this weekend means a lot to me. I haven't seen you girls since last September at the Sea Glass House," she replies.

We drop off our shopping packages and head to the elevator.

"Hello, Mathew," I say.

"Good evening, ladies. The limo driver has just arrived and is waiting for you at the entrance to the Plaza," he says.

"Thank you, Mathew," I say.

"Mathew, you better get some rest. There will be six of us tonight, and we are a rough crowd," Mary Beth squeals as we enter the elevator.

I did ask the girls to pack lightly so they would not have to check their luggage. Mary Beth, Nancy, and I meet the limo driver down at the front lobby.

"Good evening. My name is Andrew, and I will be your driver for the next few days," he says.

"Good eve-nin'," says Mary Beth with a southern drawl. I can't seem to take her anywhere.

"Hello, Andrew. I'm Sara Springs. How long do you think it will take us to get to the airport?" I ask.

"We should be there within thirty to forty minutes," the driver replies.

"Good. My friends' flight is arriving at four thirty, and we should be there right on schedule to pick them up," I say.

We get into the limo, and off we go to La Guardia. I always wonder about the amount of traffic in New York City. As we turn the corner off Broadway, a bright yellow taxi pulls right in front of the limo. The taxi driver gets out of his car and comes up to the limo. Mary Beth and I are shocked. Andrew, the driver, gets out of the limo and faces the cab driver.

"What do you think you are doing pulling out in front of my cab?" the cabbie yells.

"Listen, buddy, I had the light; you were supposed to stop," Andrew replies.

"You think you are tough, don't you, limo driver?" says the cabbie.

"Get in your cab and get out of my way, or I will push you and your cab up onto the sidewalk," Andrew says without raising his voice. "These ladies need to get to the airport, and I intend to get them there and on time," he adds.

The cabbie bows up at Andrew. Andrew grabs the cab driver's arms and pulls them back and around the driver's back. He then pushes the cabbie back to his yellow cab, says a few words which Mary Beth, Nancy, and I couldn't hear, and opens the door to the cab. The driver looks scared and gets back into his cab. He speeds off with his tires burning rubber.

Andrew says, "Sorry, ladies, I had to straighten that guy out. No problems now. Sit back and enjoy your ride."

"Whew," Mary Beth says.

"New York City, girl," I say.

"This is normal New York traffic," Nancy says, laughing.

We drive to the flight arrival area and see the girls coming out of the sliding doors. I open the limo's sunroof and yell, "Over here, girls! Lizzy, we are over here!"

"There they are!" yells Lizzy as she points to the limo.

I see Lizzy and Cici but not Elle.

"Where is Elle?" I ask with an exhausted look on my face.

Lizzy responds, "You know you told us not to bring everything we owned? Well..."

Here comes Elle with two of the largest pieces of luggage one has ever seen.

"What the..." I say. "Did you bring everything you own?" I ask.

Elle giggles and drags her luggage to the limo. Andrew picks up both pieces of luggage and places them in the trunk with the other ladies' luggage. Reminder, don't take Elle on any long trips.

"Where to ladies?" asks Andrew.

"Back to the Plaza for tonight," I say.

"You know I am available to you for the next three days," says Andrew.

"Tonight, we will have dinner at the Plaza and do some walking around Times Square. Tomorrow, we would like to be picked up at nine. We are going to the Statute of Liberty, then lunch at the Modern restaurant outside the Museum of Modern Art, and in the afternoon, we would like to tour New York on one of those double-decker buses," I say.

"That sounds great. You, ladies, are in for a full day of adventure. I will be here at nine sharp," Andrew replies.

We arrive at the Plaza, the porter takes the luggage, and I head to the reservation desk to pick up the extra card keys. I give the porter our keys, and we get into the elevator.

"This is so beautiful," says Elle.

"Thank you so much for this weekend. I am so excited. I have never been to New York City!" exclaims Cici.

"Thanks, Sara. You didn't have to do this for us, but I am glad you did," says Lizzy.

The elevator opens, and there is Mathew with a big smile.

"Ladies, I have a special treat just for you. After you drop off your luggage, please come to the dining room," he says.

"Thank you, Mathew. We will be right back," I say.

The girls have the porters drop their luggage off. We go to the dining room.

"Oh my Gawd," whispers Cici. "This is fantastic."

"Mathew, this is incredible; you are too much," Mary Beth says, kissing Mathew's cheek.

Mathew has set up a lovely buffet of "bald" shrimp, BBQ meatballs, cheeses, fruit, an assortment of bread, and pastries galore. He even has little bags of chocolate for each of us to take to our rooms. He opens a couple of bottles of wine and pours us each a glass.

"I heard this was a get-away weekend for you ladies. I had to make it a perfect first evening," says Mathew.

"Wow, this is a perfect first evening!" says Elle as she picks up a beautiful china dish and places several shrimp upon it.

"A limo to pick us up at the airport, an amazing hotel and room, and this!" squeals Lizzy. "What a way to vaca," she adds.

We enjoy our food and wine, and spend time catching up on families and life. After a couple of hours of socializing, we decide to walk to Times Square. Times Square is an amazing place. People are lined up to purchase tickets to the shows, automobiles are bumper to bumper, and tourists are pouring in and out of the shops, purchasing souvenirs to take back home. Mary Beth catches the eye of the underwear-singing cowboy, and he moves closer to our group. Elle, Cici, and Mary Beth put some dollars into the guitar lying against the cowboy's leg. Of course, we all get a picture of him on our cell phones. Weston will get a kick out of this one.

Lizzy sees a bar, and off we go. When in New York, do as the Yorkers do. The girls head into the bar, and Cici locates a table in the back. I don't know how she sees it because the bar is dark, and the lights are flickering on and off. The music is not bad, more like a mix of pop and rap. The bass is popping, and my hips are moving in sync with the music.

"I would like a vodka and orange juice, light on the vodka," I say.

Cici orders a margarita, and Nancy orders a diet Coke. Mary Beth, Elle, and Lizzy order skinny Pina coladas.

"What do you ladies think about New York so far?" I ask.

Cici responds, "It is just like I thought it would be, busy and fascinating."

"I love it so far. I feel like I am in a dream," says Elle stretching her long legs out in front of her chair.

The rest of us have been to New York before, but not in this social standing. I enjoy watching everyone having a good time and know tomorrow will be even more exciting.

At noon, we head back to the hotel and into our rooms.

"Did you see anyone following us?" asks Mary Beth.

"No; after the airport pick up, I didn't see anyone," I say.

“Maybe, he realized that we are here for a girls’ weekend and will leave us alone,” says Mary Beth.

“We keep this to ourselves, right Mary Beth?” I ask.

“Yes, there is no reason to tell them,” she says.

Chapter Thirty-One

The next morning, I walk out onto the balcony with my coffee and blanket to enjoy the view. Lizzy is on the next balcony, wrapped up like an Eskimo, reading and drinking coffee.

"Good morning, Lizzy," I say.

"Good morning, my dear," replies Lizzy.

"Did you sleep well?" I ask.

"Yes, I was so tired that I went straight to sleep," answers Lizzy. "The Pina colada definitely made me relax," she adds.

"I need to talk to you today. Mary Beth and I found out some information that I want to share with you. When we go on the bus ride this afternoon, sit with me. I will fill you in then, okay?" I say.

"Okay," she replies as Elle opens the door to the balcony.

"Good morning, you two. I love this weather. Back home, it is still in the seventies in the morning. I just saw the local weather; it is supposed to snow tonight in New York," she says with her face beaming.

"That's great. This city is so beautiful when it snows. The last time Weston and I visited, it snowed. Everything looked so clean and heavenly," I say. "Tonight, I have something special planned for dinner," I add.

"Everything is so perfect; what else could you do to make it more special?" asks Elle.

"You'll see," I say, grinning.

I glance at my watch and see that it is eight o'clock. "It's eight o'clock. We better get ready. The limo is picking us up at nine, and we still need to dress and grab a bite in the dining room," I say.

I go inside the suite and find Mary Beth dressed and ready for the day. She is wearing brown boots, black jeans, and a plaid brown and black turtle neck sweater. She grabs her purse and black quilted jacket. She yells, going out the door, "I'll meet you, ladies, in the dining room."

"By yourself?" I ask.

"No, Mathew will be there," she says with a wink of her eye.

"Mathew is not your friend! He is paid to be nice to you!" I yell as she closes the door to our suite.

I dress in my blue jeans, ivory knitted sweater, and blue suede boots. Got to love Elvis' "Blue Suede Shoes." I grab my brown puffy jacket with the hood and head to the dining room. Mary Beth, Lizzy, Nancy, and Cici are sitting at a table, drinking coffee and eating bagels.

"Hello, everyone," I say. "Where is Elle?" I ask.

"You know Elle; she can't decide among the ten sweaters she brought with her," says Lizzy.

It is already eight forty-five. At eight fifty-five in walks Elle.

"Sorry, guys, I couldn't decide what I wanted to wear," she says, grabbing a to-go cup of coffee and a bagel.

We all get up from the table and head for the elevator. "Have a nice day, ladies," says Mathew.

Once outside the hotel, I notice Andrew waiting for us. "Good morning, ladies. Are you ready for your adventure?" he asks.

"Yes!" we all yell in unison.

"Okay, first stop the boat to the Statute of Liberty," says Andrew. "Ms. Springs, we need to talk, please."

"What's up, Andrew?" I ask.

"I saw a man following us to the airport last night. He was a big Italian guy. I didn't notice him again after that. Are you okay?" asks Andrew.

"We're fine. Please keep a watch out for him today, Andrew," I say.

"Sure, I will watch out for you ladies," responds Andrew.

We all gather inside the limo. As our car star moving, everyone looks out the windows at the astonishing New York skyscrapers. We have a few in Jacksonville, but nothing like this city. The limo pulls up to the marina while we are all in awe at the amazing statute awaiting us on the small island. I imagine my ancestors on the ships that brought them over from England and Wales. This is where my family's American adventure began.

We get out of the limo, and Andrew says, "Enjoy yourselves. I will be waiting here when you get back. Call on your way back, and I will pick you up at the disembarking ramp."

"Will do," I say.

"Bye," we all say.

Once we embark on the boat and head up to the top deck so that we can get the best view, I say, "Ladies, we should probably not stay more than a couple of hours as our reservations at Modern are at twelve, and we don't want to miss it."

Elle, Nancy, Mary Beth, and Lizzy give me a thumbs up, and Cici says, "A'wright."

The walk around the Statute of Liberty was inspirational. I notice tears in Cici's eyes and ask, "Are you okay?"

"Yes, I was just thinking about my son's service in the military and what it meant to me. He was a truly remarkable young man," she says.

I grab her by the hand, and we continue our walk. We meet Nancy at the immigration computers with her staring at one of the monitors.

"I just found my great, great, great uncle. He came over on a steamship from London. I knew he was the first of our family to come over, but I had never seen it in writing before. Here it is; he came over with a wife and two small boys."

It was a somber morning. After boarding the boat, we all hug and huddle by the railings, lost in our own thoughts. I call Andrew to tell him we will be the next boat to disembark. I see the limo and point it out to the girls.

"Who is ready for lunch?" I ask.

"I am," says Nancy.

"Me too," says Elle. "That bagel is long gone," she adds.

"Andrew, get us to the Modern. We are all starving," I say.

The Beach Girls load into the limo, and Andrew presses his foot on the gas pedal. We pull into the Modern's driveway and exit the limo.

"Sara, please call when you are ready to leave. I will park the limo around the block and wait. Enjoy your lunch, ladies," says Andrew.

"Will do," I say, and we head into the restaurant.

The hostess seats us at a table near the Museum of Modern Art's indoor gardens. I pick a seat facing the gardens and notice the beautiful flowers. There are all colors of blooms and flowers I have never seen before. It feels like spring!

The waiter arrives, and we order drinks. We really aren't big drinkers, but this is a special holiday for us, and we are enjoying every minute of it.

"I'll have a pineapple juice, orange juice, and vodka mixed drink with a cherry," I say.

"That would be our citrus ice martini," she says.

"Yes, I would like a citrus ice martini," I say with a smirk. In Florida, we just tell the bartender what we want. No questions asked; just a reply of "Yes, ma'am."

The other girls order wine spritzers, and we all ask for ice water. Every drink in Florida has ice cubes. Perhaps ice costs more up north; just saying. The waitress brings our drinks, and we toast the weekend.

"Here's to great friends and Beach Girls' weekend," I say.

"Cheers!" we all say as we click our glasses together.

I order a Cobb salad with strawberries and mandarin oranges. I am a citrus kind of girl, a true Floridian. Mary Beth orders fried calamari and a side garden salad, while Lizzy orders a chicken salad croissant. Cici orders 'wangs' (wings, I translate for the waitress). Elle and Nancy order shrimp salad croissants.

The food arrives; it is delicious. The waitress adds fresh bacon bits and ground pepper to my salad and brings a basket of hard rolls with creamy butter. As soon as we finish lunch, I call Andrew and head to the tour bus terminal. It is so cold, so we all buy a pair of mittens and knitted scarfs from the vendor table near the bus terminal.

Our bus is two-tiered, but since it is so cold out, Lizzy and I sit inside toward the back of the bus. The driver begins to move the bus toward Fifth Avenue. The store fronts are elaborately decorated for the spring even though it is only forty degrees outside and dropping. Easter parade hats in various styles and colors adorn the shop windows, along with stuffed Easter bunnies and baskets.

The driver says, "We are now heading to Harlem."

"Yes, Harlem."

Lizzy immediately says, "I have got to get off. I need a bathroom."

"What!?' I say.

"Now!" she states as she pulls the emergency cord of the bus. I am not letting her off in Harlem by herself, so I jump off with her, racing to keep up.

"We will meet you back at the hotel!" I yell, chasing Lizzy into a Mexican restaurant.

She goes in, yells "bano," and heads to the bathroom. I go to a table and sit. It is really creepy in here. The place smells of old grease, and the tables are old and rickety. An old Mexican guy comes to the table and says, "Menu?"

I, remembering very little from my college Spanish classes, reply, "See."

He hands me a menu and moves over to the counter. I look at the menu and recognize huevos (eggs) and toceno (bacon). I wave the man over and order, "Dos huevos and tres el toceno." I didn't know how to say toast, so I just ordered coffee.

A few minutes later, the old man serves eggs, bacon, tortillas, and café. I try to eat slowly since I have no idea what is happening to Lizzy. Sometimes she has a bowel attack and has even jumped out of the car in Savannah to run to the nearest restroom. That is another story. I ask for another cup of café and drink it slowly. Finally, Lizzy comes out of the back and grabs my arm. I throw a twenty on the table and hurry with her.

"What the heck is wrong with you?" I ask.

"Why didn't you come to check on me?" she asks.

"Come check on you? I was scared. I ordered another breakfast and drank two more cups of coffee. I didn't know where you were or if you were even alive," I say.

We sit down at the bus stop across from the Mexican restaurant. It was covered with "Friday the Thirteenth Part XIII" posters.

"I had to poop so badly; I barely made it to the restroom Then, there was no toilet paper. I kept yelling for you, but you never came. I had to use my underwear and throw it in the trash," said Lizzy.

I laughed so hard that I cried. "I'm sorry," I said. "I was so scared. There were two men in there, and they kept looking at me with grins on their faces. I thought we were going to be taken as sex slaves," I say.

This time Lizzy is laughing, "Yeah, that's just what they would want; us as sex slaves. Wait until someone cleans that bathroom"

Suddenly, we hear a tiny voice coming from one of the barred windows above the restaurant.

"Help me, help me," the voice said.

Lizzy and I get up really fast and take off down the road to the safer part of town. We walk six blocks and turn left on a pretty road of brownstone houses. We are feeling much better, and Lizzy asks, "What did you want to tell me this morning?"

"It is nothing," I say, knowing I should inform Lizzy, but I am not ready. I need to think about this some more.

"Okay, I know you will tell me when you are ready. Just, please, be careful," says Lizzy.

"I told Mary Beth not to say anything. Maybe I will tell everyone on Sunday morning before we fly home," I say.

"Look, Broadway!" Lizzy yells.

We turn onto Broadway making our way back to the Plaza. We enter the building and head into the elevator. Once we make it to our floor, Mathew is waiting for us.

"Hello, ladies, where are your friends?" he asks.

"Oh, they will be here shortly. They are still out sightseeing," I say.

"Is there wine in the dining room?" asks Lizzy.

"Yes, ma'am," says Mathew.

We enter the dining room; Lizzy grabs a bottle of opened wine and a glass.

"Out of here. I have got to take a shower and clean up before I meet the girls," she says.

I decide to sit by the window overlooking Times Square. Lost in thoughts, I hear, "Hey Sara, glad y'all made it back?" I look down from the balcony and see the girls arrive in the limo and wave to them

The Beach Girls and Lizzy join me in the lounge a few minutes later. Lizzy tells them all about our adventure. There is lots of laughing and giggling. To hear it again is funny; I can just imagine the look on the face of the person who has to clean that restroom. Bless their little heart.

"Ladies, look outside! It is snowing!" I yell as we all rush to the windows. "Let's go to our rooms' balconies," I add.

"Let's go!" says Elle.

Running back to our rooms and pushing Mathew aside, I couldn't help but giggle like a school girl. I rush into the room and open the door to the balcony. Mary Beth is right on my heels, squealing. Florida girls don't get to see snow that often. It has been snowing so hard that it covered the balcony in a brilliant white blanket. The other girls arrive on their balconies, and we all do a "snow dance." We dance a little, jumping with our hands in the air, swinging like we don't care. Everyone has their cell phones out and is taking pictures of the beautiful sight. What a wonderful time to be with good friends.

I call the girls, "Hey, y'all meet me in our room; I have a surprise for you!"

A few minutes later, they all arrive in the room. "What's this surprise?" asks Mary Beth, having no idea what I will share. I can't wait to tell them.

Chapter Thirty-Two

"Tonight, we are all going on a horse and buggy ride in the snow through Central Park. We will dine at the Tavern on the Green!" I yell.

"Wow!" exclaim Elle and Cici as they rush to give me a bear hug.

"Mary Beth, breathe!" I yell as I slap her on the back. I knew this would be a big surprise for her. A few years back, Mary Beth and I came to New York for her birthday, and we surprised her with dinner at the Tavern. She cried most of the night because she was so excited and happy.

"Lizzy, get her some water," says Nancy.

Lizzy gets a water bottle from the ice bucket containing spring water bottles on the living area table and hands it to Mary Beth. She drinks a little and lets out a loud "Alright! I have always wanted to go back there. It has been closed for a while. I didn't know it had opened back up for diners."

"Okay, be ready at six; the horses and buggies will wait at the front entrance. Be sure to dress in layers since it is not going to be above freezing tonight," I say, heading to the bathroom to shower.

Tonight, in front of the Plaza, are three white carriages with six strong, brown steeds. The carriage drivers stand beside the horses as we separate into pairs. The men are wearing long, black, woolen coats and wool top hats. Each man has a colored scarf wrapped around his neck. Lizzy and I step into the first carriage, and our driver covers our laps with a heavy, red-velvet blanket that matches his scarf.

"Thank you," I say.

Cici and Nancy get into the second carriage while Elle and Mary Beth grab the handle of their carriage, lift themselves up, and snuggle in for the ride. The snowflakes float from the sky like crystals on a chandelier. The carriage drivers snap their whips, and our ride begins.

"This is like a fairy tale. I feel like Cinderella going to the ball," says Lizzy.

"Me too," I say leaning back into the warm leather seat of the carriage. We ride along to the clippity, cloppity sounds of the horses' hoofs as they hit the paved road. Lights twinkle in the old oak trees, and the cold wind flows across our rosy cheeks. The scenery makes our adventure even more exciting. I hear a giggle coming from Cici in the carriage behind us and turn around to see her pointing at two squirrels on an oak branch, humping like they needed to get warm. Leave it to Cici to notice two squirrels getting it on instead of a snow-covered landscape with twinkling lights. I look at Lizzy and say, "I guess they were cold."

Mary Beth has her tongue sticking out, trying to catch a few snowflakes, and Elle is making a video of the carriage ride. It is strange when one gets with their friends, they act like children. Such is life!

We arrive at the Tavern on the Green, and the doorman hustles to help me out of the carriage. The Tavern resembles a fairy house with sparkling lights and fairy dust falling from the sky. The trees' limbs are covered with crystalized snowflakes, and the blanket makes me feel warm and cozy.

"This is incredible," I say.

"You picked the perfect day to visit," says the doorman, gently holding my hand.

"I have never seen the Tavern look so beautiful," says Nancy.

Cici picks up a handful of snow, mashes it into a ball, and throws it at Nancy's head. "Take that, sister," she says.

Nancy grabs Cici and pushes her into a heap of snow piled up next to the road beside the carriages. The girls both laugh, and the rest of us start snapping pictures with our cell phones. Nancy yells, "Those better not be put on Facebook or Twitter!"

We all laugh, place our phones into our purses, and head into the Tavern. I look back at the doorman, "Can't take them anywhere," I say as he laughs and waves.

Inside the Tavern, I see more twinkling lights and vines growing along the ceiling and walls. I feel like I have just stepped into an enchanted garden. The elegantly dressed young hostess meets us at the entrance to the dining rooms. "Welcome, ladies. Do you have reservations with us this evening," she asks.

"Yes. The reservations will be under Sara Springs." I respond, smiling.

"Yes, ma'am. Mrs. Springs, we have your table ready in our Fremont Room overlooking Central Park. Please, right this way," says the hostess as she leads us to our table. "Your waiter will be right with you ladies. Please enjoy your dining experience," she adds.

"Isn't this place beautiful? Look over there! I think that is George Clooney," says Mary Beth.

We all quickly turn our heads in her direction but only see a man in a hat and long coat.

"Mary Beth, I don't see George," I say.

"Well, I know that was him," Mary Beth says.

"Look at all the lights and the candles on the tables; they are magical," says Elle.

"It really is beautiful," I say, gazing around at the beautiful decorations.

The waiter arrives at our table with two bottles of champaign, the expensive kind.

"Good evening, ladies. My name is Jack, and I will be serving you tonight. Mr. Springs has asked that we treat you, ladies, very special while you are dining. He has a card for you, Mrs. Springs," Jack says, handing me the card.

I read aloud, "Please enjoy your champaign and your trip. Have fun, and remember that whatever happens in New York needs to stay there. Love to all my sweet friends and my lady."

"Ah, Weston is so sweet," says Elle.

Mary Beth adds, "He is a keeper, Sara."

Jack pours us each a glass of champagne, and we all raise our glasses for a toast.

"Here's to Weston, wonderful friends, and more great days to come!" announces Elle as she eyes Jack.

"Here, Here! Great days to come," I say.

The waiter returns to the table with a silver basket of yeast rolls and soft honey-butter wrapped in a warm cloth. The waiter behind Victor gently sets menus in front of each of us. As we gaze through the menu, another waiter comes by our table carrying plates of huge cuts of prime rib and baked potatoes to the table next to ours. I look at Mary Beth, and her eyes are wide open. She wasn't even blinking. She looks over at me and shakes her head for "yes." She and I both love prime rib and often we split dinners.

"Mary Beth, let's split a prime rib dinner," I say.

"Yes, let's do that," she replies.

I order the prime rib medium with two loaded baked potatoes and two Caesar salads. Lizzy and Cici order the grilled trout almandine with mixed vegetables and a side salad each. Elle and Nancy order the fillet mignons rare.

"Our show tonight is Hamilton, and it starts at eight. I have box seats for us near the stage. It is now six-thirty, so we should be right on time," I say.

"Yes, if we leave here by seven-thirty, we should be seated at the Barrymore Theatre before the curtain goes up," says Nancy. "Is the limo picking us up?" she adds.

"Yes, Andrew will be waiting outside for us," I reply.

"Hey, y'all, did you see those crazy squirrels in the oak tree doing the nasty?" asks Cici.

"I did and thought they were going to fall out of that old tree," said Elle.

"I was so busy looking at the incredible landscape of snow and twinkling lights to notice any squirrels," says Lizzy.

"Me too. Between the good-looking carriage driver and the snow, I missed the squirrels," states Mary Beth.

"Imagine what heaven must look like if it is this beautiful on Earth," sighs Nancy. "This is what I love about New York City; we have all the seasons," she adds.

Our food arrives carried out by three waiters as if a Broadway production has been arranged. First, our salads; each in a small bowl placed inside a larger bowl of ice to keep the salad chilled. Beside each salad, the waiter places a small, silver dressing pitcher. The next waiter sprinkles cheese and ground pepper on each salad. The third waiter brings a platter of delicious cheeses and more yeast rolls with soft honey butter.

"Can I get you, ladies, anything else," asks the third waiter.

"No, this is fabulous," I say.

The three waiters head back to the kitchen. The conversations stop, and the eating begins. After fifteen minutes, Jack, the head waiter, and four other waiters bring out the prime rib, trout, and fillets. Each waiter serves their plates and returns to the kitchen.

"Amazing, this prime rib is perfectly cooked. It is so tender that I can cut it with my butter knife," I say.

"Yummy," says Mary Beth placing another juicy, garlic-crusted piece of prime rib into her mouth.

"How's the trout?" I ask Cici and Lizzy.

"Great. The vegetables are delicious; the chef has added something to them that I can't make out," Cici says.

"The chef cooks the best steaks in New York. The DEA has our night meetings here once a month, and the steak is my favorite," says Nancy. "The Tavern has smaller dining rooms for meetings and small conferences," she adds.

"Usually, I have to send my steak back to the kitchen to be cooked some more, but this one is prepared perfectly," says Elle.

We finish our meals and the two bottles of champagne. Jack returns to the table and asks, "Would you ladies like dessert?"

"Do you have crème brulee?" asks Mary Beth. Where ever she goes, Mary Beth asks for crème brulee. I can always enjoy a good crème brulee too.

"Yes, we do, along with a chocolate lava cake and an almond torte," says Jack.

"I'll have the crème brulee," says Mary Beth.

"Me too," I say.

"I'll have the lava cake," says Lizzy.

"I'll have the almond torte," says Elle.

"Nothing for me," says Nancy.

"No, thank you; too many carbs and sugar. Those are not good for your circulation," adds Cici.

"I am on vacation, and I don't care if it has a million carbs and sugar," says Mary Beth.

"Here, here," I add.

At seven-thirty, I pay the check and leave a hefty tip. The wait staff is superb, and all the Beach Girls have a great time. Feeling happy that they were all smiling, I gather the group and head out to the limo. Andrew is waiting to open our doors. The snow has slowed, and the road no longer looks frozen.

"Off to Hamilton at the Barrymore Theatre, Andrew," I say. "Can I ask you to pick up six lattes while we are at the show and have them for us when you drive us home after the show?" I ask.

"Ms. Sara, I would be delighted to have them waiting in the limo when you ladies return tonight," says Andrew. He will get a big tip for that.

We arrive at the theatre, and Andrew opens our doors. I head up to the all-call window to pick up our tickets and hand each lady one. We walk through the theatre lobby and meet the hall porter, a beautiful young lady. It seems like the city is full of pretty girls.

"May I take a look at your tickets, please," she says. "Follow me," she instructs us, and we follow her up two flights of stairs to our box.

The box contains six armchairs with velvet, plush cushions that must be six inches in height and made of soft feathers. I know feathers because I see a couple poking out of the side of the cushion. The box is angled toward the stage, which couldn't be more than ten feet from us. Next to each chair is a tiny table for drinks. A waiter comes through the curtains of our box to take our drink orders.

After we receive our drinks, the lights go down. I see Mary Beth and Lizzy reach into their purses and pull out binoculars.

"Girls, we are only a few feet away from the stage," I say. "Put those away," I add.

"I don't want to miss anything, and you know what I mean," says Mary Beth winking at me.

"I agree," says Lizzy with a grin on her face.

I shake my head and turn toward the stage. Thank goodness there is no one but the actors who can see us.

At intermission, a waiter arrives at our box. "Would you ladies like another drink from the bar?" he asks.

"Yes, I would like two bottles of champagne and six glasses," I say. We might as well end the show with a toast.

After a few minutes, the waiter arrives with our champagne and fills our glasses.

"I would like to toast Sara for bringing us along on the adventure," says Lizzy.

"To Sara," everyone says in unison.

"Thank you, my friends. You all make me happy, too," I say.

"That was a fantastic play," says Lizzy. "Especially the way that tall actor in the top hat looks," she adds.

"You noticed him too," says Mary Beth laughing.

We clap and stand for the ovation. This is one night we won't forget soon. It will be a topic of discussion for years to come at the beach house. It snowed while we were inside at the play. As we exit the doorway, Andrew is waiting right outside the theatre. He opens our door, and we slide in. The fresh aroma of the lattes fills the air.

"I will definitely bring my husband to see Hamilton," says Nancy.

As we ride back to the Plaza, Cici says, yawning, "I am really tired, y'all. I get up every day at six and need my beauty sleep. Before we go in, I would like Andrew to take a picture of us making snow angels."

We arrive at the entrance to the hotel lobby, and Andrew opens the limo door. "Okay, hand over the cell phones, and I will take your pictures," he says.

We run to the nearest pile of snow, lie down, and make snow angels. "Take the pictures, Andrew! It is freezing," I say, laughing. Luckily, the security guard did not see us until the pictures were taken. We saw him coming and jumped up out of the snow. The other ladies ran into the hotel, laughing and brushing snow off their clothes. I stand next to six feet six inches tall Andrew for safety. The security guard, seeing us, turns around and heads back toward the hotel. I really think, after looking at Andrew, he decided it wasn't worth it.

"Did anyone follow us tonight?" I curiously ask Andrew.

"No, I haven't seen anyone suspicious at all," says Andrew. "Don't worry; enjoy your trip with your friends. I will watch out for you ladies. What time will you need the limo tomorrow?" he asks.

"Let's make it around ten in the morning. I think we need a little more rest tonight," I say.

We meet in the hotel lobby, gather in the elevator, and make our way to our rooms.

"Good night, ladies," says Cici.

"Good night, all," says Elle and Nancy simultaneously.

"Good night, John Boy," I say as I open the door to the suite. I hear a few giggles out in the hallway. I head to my room and dress for bed. After a few minutes of lying in bed and reminiscing about the night's events, I fall fast asleep.

Chapter Thirty-Three

The next morning I wake up at about eight o'clock. The snow had stopped so I can go outside on the balcony. I grab a blanket, a cup of coffee, and the New York Times. Cici, Nancy, and Lizzy were already up.

"Good morning, my lovelies," I say, noticing that Cici and Nancy look like the homeless people one sees by the subway station. The ladies' blankets were wrapped around their heads, along with woolen caps. The new mittens which they purchased earlier were wrapping their chilled hands.

"Good morning, Sara," they reply.

"Cici, is that your moose hat from Christmas brunch?" I ask. Cici has a large knitted moose hat with ears hanging down to her knees. The tall antlers on top light up the hat with white lights. She looks hilarious and sweet at the same time.

"Yes, it is," she answers with a grin.

"Lord, girl, you are something," I say.

"What's happening today?" asks Lizzy wrapping the blanket tighter around her face.

Nancy gets up, gives me a wave, and rushes inside, "It is too cold out here," she says.

"We need to meet in the dining room at nine-thirty. The limo will be downstairs at ten o'clock. I am taking all of you to one of my favorite places, The American Museum of Natural History. You will love this place," I say.

At nine-thirty, we meet in the dining room. I opt for the bacon and eggs with whole wheat toast. The bagels were causing a ruckus in my digestive system. The other girls hit the buffet for sausage, eggs, and whole wheat toast. Cici eats fruit and sneaks a small Danish roll into her purse, thinking no one is looking.

"Did everyone sleep well last night?" I ask.

"I know I did. We had a full day yesterday," says Lizzy.

"We sure did. I don't use up that much energy at the hospital," says Cici.

"I slept like a baby. I wish I had this bed at home," says Elle.

"You could if you sold your new car," says Nancy smiling.

Chapter Thirty-Four

Andrew is waiting for us at the limo. "Good morning, ladies. I understand you will be visiting the American Museum of Natural History today," he says.

"Yes, we are," says Lizzy.

"I am so excited," says Elle.

"I want to see one of them big dinosaurs," says Cici as she slowly moves toward the limo door.

We drive through the city and arrive at the museum. We walk up the many steps of the entrance. The ticket counter is to its right. I had purchased our tickets online, and they were ready at the window. Once we receive our tickets, we are ready to check our coats.

"The coat check-in is right down the hall on the left side," says the ticket collector.

"Thank you," I say, and we move down the hall to check the coats. The museum has three floors, and we don't want to drag our heavy coats with us. Removing that coat feels amazing. The museum is warm, and Florida women in their late fifties can't stand the heat. At home, we have our HVAC repairmen on speed dial. When the electricity goes out during a hurricane, we make reservations at the Omni Hotel. We may like to live in Florida, but we don't really like the heat, humidity, or sweat.

The ladies walk back to the center of the museum and glance up at a huge Saurischian dinosaur.

"Did you know that the first dinosaurs had feathers?" I ask the girls.

"No, did they fly?" asks Cici.

"Yes, they are called pterosaurs," I say. "My students and I read an article in our reading program about these dinosaurs during our reading class. It was interesting; the kids enjoyed the article," I add.

"That's cool," says Elle. "Look at that! I have never seen a dinosaur skeleton so big," she adds.

"I wonder how big his...?" Mary Beth whispers.

"Move on, ladies; we have a lot to see," I say.

We take the escalator to the next floor to the Hall of Gems and Minerals. I walk into the hall and see a huge amethyst geode. Amethyst geodes are formed inside the earth.

"This reminds me of the amethyst I mined in North Carolina a few years back. I had the stone cut and made into a ring for my mother," I say. "I read that there are over five thousand, five hundred specimens in this exhibit. This is so amazing," I continue viewing the stones.

"I think I'll take that ten-carat diamond over there," says Mary Beth. "You think we can put it in my purse," she adds. "Do you remember the huge golden nugget we saw at the Cody Museum in Cody, Wyoming?" Mary Beth asks.

"Yes, it would probably take all of that gold to make a ring big enough to hold the diamond," I say.

"Did you know it takes millions of years for these gems to form?" asks Cici.

"No, how do you know that?" I ask.

"I read it here on this sign," she says, giggling.

I roll my eyes skyward, and we move to the caveman exhibit in the Human Evolution area.

"I wouldn't want to mate with that," says Mary Beth, and we all laugh.

"He kind of looks like Kevin Costner," I say, knowing I would get a rise from the girls.

"Don't go there," says Lizzy. "My man, Kevin, does not look like an ape-man. He is a modern-day species of the male gender. And a fine one at that," she adds.

We leave the ape-man and Kevin behind us and move on to the "Industrial Revolution." The first exhibit we see is of the cotton gin, and then an exhibit of women working on an assembly line.

"I'm glad we didn't have to work on the assembly lines back in the day," says Nancy. "The DEA is a lot more fun and exciting. Just last week, we uncovered a ton of cocaine being shipped by a sugar and flour cargo ship. We are still looking for the drug lords," adds Nancy.

"That is exciting. Last week at my high school, the county cops arrested eight students for possession of marijuana and for selling crack. One of the boys had a secret compartment under the back bed of his truck containing a hundred pounds of pot. The cops picked up his drug-dealing dad and grandpa that morning before coming to our school. His momma is already in jail for drugs. These children have a hard time growing up," I say.

"Yes, drugs are so bad these days. Last week in the ER, we had a thirteen-year-old die on our table. He had been stabbed twelve times in the chest. Apparently, seven boys, ages ten to fourteen, were fighting over drugs, and two of the boys pulled out knives. These kids are just babies," says Cici.

"I wonder where the parents were; probably in the bedroom stoned out of their heads," I say.

We move along to the "Worlds Beyond" space section of the museum. An old rocket ship hangs overhead from wires. Right in the middle of the circular room is a glass box about the size of a large packing box you can get at the UPS store. It sits on a four feet tall pedestal. Inside two sides of the box are openings large enough to place your hands. Inside the glass box is a large piece of moon rock.

"Wow! Look at the moon rock. You can actually touch it with your hand," I say.

The other girls rush over and take turns sticking their hands inside the box. I take their pictures with my phone when no one is looking. I notice that Cici's hand is still inside the box. She has a troubled look on her face; she can't get her hand out of the box. The lights start flashing as two security guards come running into the room They rush over to Cici and she starts crying. "My hand is stuck, my hand is stuck!" Please don't shoot me!"

The other Beach Girls gather near her to ensure she isn't shot. We form a ring around her protecting her from the guards. "It is a mistake! She has large hands, is all!" I cry out, still holding my position around Cici.

"Ma'am, what's going on here?" asks one of the guards.

We slowly move away from Cici. "I got my hand stuck when I was touching the moon rock. I can't get it out," says Cici.

"Sir, I am a DEA agent, and this is my friend from Florida," says Nancy pulling out her badge. "She placed her hand into the hole and is now stuck. Is there any way you can get her hand out?" she asks. Cici is still crying.

"Let me get the key, and I will get your hand out of there, ma'am," says the second guard. The guard walks over to a security box, opens it, and removes a set of keys.

People are gathering around us and ogling Cici. "There is no need to ogle. I just got my hand stuck with the moon rock. You might not want to try this. I am a nurse and can tell you that you will get cramps in your hand if you do," she says very calmly.

"When we get your hand out of the box, I want you to leave the building," says the first guard.

"First of all, she didn't do anything wrong. Your box holes are too small for her hands. We will leave when we are ready," I say, not happy with the guard.

"I want to see the ocean exhibit," says Elle. "I heard it was amazing."

"We will leave after the ocean exhibit, and you may escort us if you would like," I say.

After the ocean exhibit, I turn to the guard. "We are finished visiting today and are all leaving. I will call Andrew, our driver, and have him pick us up," I say.

I stand near the exit door, hoping that Cici doesn't get caught in anything else. I take the disc with the picture of the guard placing the key in the hole, releasing her hand, and place it into my coat pocket. I will be using this picture and story in the future. How many people get kicked out of the best museum in the country?

"Over here; let's go," I say.

Once again, Andrew is waiting by the limo.

"I heard someone got their hand stuck in the moon rock exhibit. Let me guess; it is either Cici or Mary Beth," says Andrew.

"I heard that, and no, it was not me," says Mary Beth with a smirk on her face.

Cici looks down at the pavement, holding an ice bag on her wrist. "It was me," she whispers. "I just wanted to touch the darn thing," she adds.

"Andrew, will you please take us back to the Plaza before we get arrested for loitering?" I ask.

"Yes, ma'am," he says, trying to hold back a snicker.

Chapter Thirty-Five

Back at the hotel, we exit the car; Nancy assists Cici inside the building.

"Andrew, we have a six o'clock event. The Jersey Boys are playing at the Broadway Theatre tonight, and we would like you to pick us up at five-thirty. I think we need a little rest this afternoon after our adventure this morning at the Museum," I say.

"I will see you, ladies, at five-thirty. Get some rest and try to stay out of trouble," says Andrew, smiling.

The girls were holding the elevator door for me. Upon my arrival, Lizzy pushes the floor button, and off we go. Mathew is waiting for us and knows what happened.

"Are you alright, Cici?" Mathew squeals as he grabs her elbow and checks out her hand. "I heard the news on the police scanner and knew it had to be you," he says.

I thought small towns had the fastest grapevine for gossip. I was wrong; New York has the lead.

"I'm okay," murmurs Cici as Mathew escorts her slowly to her room.

Once they enter the suite, I hear Mathew say, "I will be right back with a new ice pack, pain meds, and snacks for you. You poor thing, get right into your bed and rest. That bad museum box shouldn't have hurt my lady."

I see Lizzy next to her suite and move closer to her and whisper, "I need to see you in my room. There is something I need to tell you."

"Give me five minutes, and I will be there," says Lizzy.

Mary Beth enters our suite, and I follow, closing the door behind me. "Mary Beth, it is time we tell Lizzy about our investigation in New York so we can be prepared when we get back home," I say.

"Are you sure you don't want to think about this a little more before we say anything?" Mary Beth asks.

"No, we need to find a way to clear this case; I am tired of all the mystery. Lizzy needs to help us make some decisions. I am not ready to tell the other girls; I don't want any harm to come to any of us," I say.

I hear a light knock on the door and let Lizzy into the suite.

"Lizzy, would you like some water or a glass of wine?" I ask.

"No, thank you. What's up with you two?" she asks.

"You know that Mary Beth and I came to New York a couple of days ahead of time. What we didn't tell anyone was that we came to investigate the Sea Glass House case. We rented a car and found the house where Sonny lived with his mother. She said that he was supposed to be down in Florida working, and he was going to stay with his friend, a cop named Franks. She is a very nice lady and has not heard from her son in weeks," I say.

Lizzy falls back on the sofa and stares at me as she contemplates her next words.

"I went looking around the house while Sara was speaking to the mother. I found a brand-new Cadillac in the garage and a strange satellite in the backyard. It was not a TV satellite because it was a small one on the roof of the brick house. There is something wrong with that picture," says Mary Beth.

"After we left the house, we went to a little Italian restaurant nearby and met a waitress that knew the deceased. She told us that Sonny worked for a concrete and cement labor union and was not a nice guy. He terrorized the kids in the neighborhood," I continue.

"We found the union hall. Sara and I went inside to check it out. The receptionist was very nice and showed us around the conference room," says Mary Beth.

"We saw pictures of the dead man and his pinkie ring. There were other men or Union bosses in pictures throughout the conference room. I advised the receptionist that my husband and I live in Tampa and that he is the business agent of his local," I say.

"The next morning, I get a call from a woman. I recognize her voice as that of the receptionist. She warned me to watch out because someone was watching me," I continue.

"We went shopping in Chelsea and saw a strange man following us. We kept him so busy in and out of the stores that he finally gave up," says Mary Beth.

"The evening we picked you ladies up at the airport, we noticed him in a black car following the limo. We haven't seen him since and I think he believes we are just some gals on a weekend show trip," I say. "Andrew has been watching out for us. We are not being followed now that you girls are here," I add.

"I can't believe you two put your lives in danger like that," says Lizzy.

"We had our stun guns and were never unaware of our surroundings," I say.

"Oh wow," says Lizzy.

"It is okay now. We are going to the theatre this evening and then to eat at Carmine's in Times Square. I don't think we have anything to worry about," I say.

"I think we need to contact Nancy's FBI friend when we get back. We know too much, and it is time for them to solve this murder. Lizzy, what do you think about setting up another meeting at your farm?" I ask.

"First, when we get home, we will gather all the girls together and fill them in on what has been going on," says Lizzy.

"I agree. Weston has a fishing trip next weekend, so I will invite everyone over Saturday evening for dinner. I know the information will be a shock to Cici," I say.

"Ok, we have a plan. No one mentions anything to Nancy. I will set up my speaker phone and tell her at the same time I tell the others. After all, if this is connected to drugs, she will want to know," I say.

"Please tell the others that we will meet in the dining room for hors d'oeuvres and a drink before heading to the theatre," I say.

Chapter Thirty-Six

We arrive at the private dining room, Mathew says in a sultry voice, "Ladies, you look exquisite. If I didn't know better, I would think you are all models for Gucci. May I seat you lovely ladies?" he asks.

"Yes, darling," says Mary Beth using her best southern drawl.

"Yes, Mathew," I say.

"Mathew, you are just too much," squeals Cici.

The girls do look fantastic, and we know it. It is our last night in New York, and we are dolled up. I have my new black leather jeans, black suede booties, and a shiny red satin blouse with a top and two unbuttoned buttons. I wear my diamond dangling earrings. Mary Beth is wearing her new red and black pants, boots, a low-cut tight sweater, and an amazing silver and crystal necklace and earring set. Lizzy has navy blue leather pants, a light blue cowl neck sweater, and brown boots. Cici has blue jeans with crystals lining the outside seams, blue suede boots, and a cream sweater with a wool scarf wrapped around her neck. Elle is wearing a wool short hounds-tooth skirt, knee-high black boots with black tights, and a cowl-neck cardigan. Nancy is wearing a pair of black wool pants, black boots, and an emerald green silk blouse. She has a multi-colored scarf wrapped around her neck. I agree with Mathew, we do look intriguing and beautiful.

After munching on boiled shrimp, lettuce wraps, and cookies, we head to the elevator.

"Did you notice all those businessmen looking at us," says Elle.

"Yes, I got a couple of numbers from the men at the back table," says Mary Beth.

"When did you go back there?" I ask.

"I thought the ladies' room was back there," says Mary Beth.

"You did not. You knew it was up front by the door because you have used it ten times since we've been here!" I exclaim

Mary Beth giggles, and the rest of the girls shake their heads in amazement. We love her, although we are still not used to her behavior.

"Our last night in New York will be fun and exciting," I say to the girls. "Andrew is waiting downstairs to take us to the theatre," I add.

Mathew meets us at the elevator and says, "Have a wonderful evening, ladies. I have seen Jersey Boys; the music is fantastic."

"Thanks, Mathew," we all say while entering the elevator.

"I hope they sing Sherry," says Lizzy.

"I hope they sing Big Girls Don't Cry," says Elle.

"I heard they sing those songs and My Boyfriend's Back," I say. "I have booked box seats for this show, too," I add.

"Yippee! We can have a dance party," squeals Cici.

"Yeah!" cries Mary Beth.

The elevator opens into the lobby of the Plaza, and we head to the limo parked right outside the doors. Andrew waves us over and opens the door.

"Good evening, ladies. You look amazing. I will have to keep a watch on you girls tonight," says Andrew as he gives us a wink.

"Thank you," I say, sliding across the supple leather seat.

We arrive at the theatre. Andrew opens our door, grabs our hands, and helps us out of the limo. Camera lights flash all around us, and tourists gather around the limo like we are rock stars. I whisper to Lizzy, "They must think we are important people. Boy, will they be surprised to learn that we are a bunch of grandmas on a girls' trip."

"Just smile and move," says Lizzy.

Andrew escorts us to the all-call counter, and I pick up the tickets. We head to the ticket porter.

"Good evening. You, ladies, will be in the Governor's Box tonight. It is our most luxurious seating area, and you will have a waiter to handle your requests," says a kind, distinguished older gentleman. He smiles, adding, "This way, ladies. You are in for an exciting and fun night." He leads us to an elevator up two floors to our box. The same velvet curtains hang on the three side walls, and six golden leather armchairs sit upon a cushy purple carpet. Next to the chairs are individual tables for the drinks.

"When I spoke to the ticket master, I did tell him that we are grandmas and that I wanted a box near the stage. I also said that we would need comfortable seating. I didn't know she thought we were eighty-year-old grandmas," I say, laughing.

The room was perfect, and I did feel special this evening. Looking at the ladies' faces, I could see they felt the same way.

The stage was only six feet away from our box. We enter the box, sit down in our comfortable chairs, and the older gentleman says, "Ladies, dancing in the box is allowed."

"I told y'all, dance party tonight," says Cici standing up and wiggling her derriere.

"Would you ladies like a glass of wine or a drink before the show begins?' the older gentleman asks.

"Yes, would you bring us two bottles of Moscato wine and six wine glasses?" I ask.

"Yes, ma'am. I would be delighted," the man replies.

A few minutes later, our wine and glasses arrive. I pour each lady a glass, and we toast. "To New York!" we all say at the same time.

The lights dim, and the curtains rise. "You're just too good to be true," sing the actors and the entire theatre sings along. This is going to be a great night.

The night is filled with dancing, laughing, and a lot of off-key singing. Nancy and Lizzy know the lyrics to every song. The Jersey Boys actors are constantly waving and smiling at us. I could tell that they love us as much as we love them

At the end of the show, the old gentleman enters our box and asks us to follow him backstage. We quickly jump out of our seats and follow. None of us have ever had the opportunity to visit backstage after a performance. We walk backstage, and the Jersey Boys actors start singing to us, "You're just too good to be true." Once they finish the song, we all gather for hugs. The young men take pictures with us and then escort us out to the awaiting limo. The men wish us a "good night," and off they go back into the theatre.

Andrew is holding our door to the limo open with a huge smile on his face. "Looks like you ladies had a good time," he says.

"Yes," we all say.

"Andrew, to the restaurant, please. We have reservations for eight-thirty," I say.

"Yes, Ms. Springs. We are on our way," says Andrew.

We arrive at Carmine's at eight-twenty-nine. Andrew parks right in front of the door, gets out of the car, and proceeds to open our door. The doorman ushers the other ladies inside the restaurant as I remain outside to speak with Andrew.

"Andrew, did you see anyone following us tonight?" I ask.

"No, ma'am. I haven't seen anyone since we picked up the other ladies at the airport," he says.

"Great. I imagine we will be here for at least a couple of hours. I'll give you a call when we are ready to go back to the hotel," I say.

"Ms. Springs, have a nice dinner and enjoy your friends. I will be keeping an eye out," says Andrew. "You ladies have nothing to worry about," he adds.

I walk into Carmine's as the hostess helps the other girls at our table. All heads are glancing our way. I know we look great, but I have never seen so many Italian men checking us out. As I walk to the table, I notice a table of four good-looking Italian men looking my way. One of the men gives me a wink, and I smile back. We, ladies, appreciate being noticed when we make an effort to look nice. Of course, tight pants, short skirts, and leather boots usually get noticed.

I turn back toward our table and widen my eyes. The man that winked at me is the murder victim's boss. I recognize the pinky ring and the face, even without the mustache. Sonny has a pinky ring just like the one the man is wearing. His face is the one I saw in a picture at the Concrete and Cement Local a few days ago.

I take a deep breath and sit between Mary Beth and Lizzy. The restaurant is dark, with lit candles on every table. There are a few dimmed overhead lights so the waiters can see where they are walking. The walls are covered with scarlet cloth wallpaper with gold embossed grape leaves, and the borders of the walls are trimmed in dark wood. The tables and chairs are made of rich mahogany with red velvet cushions. White linens cover the table tops, and white linen napkins are folded like tiny tents. The restaurant's atmosphere is definitely Italian. Grape vines wound their way around the columns separating each dining area in the building. Italian music flows out of the speakers located on the ceiling right above our table.

"Your waiter will be right with you," says the lovely Italian hostess. It is easy to understand how she got her job. She turns quickly, stops to greet the men at the other table, and returns to the hostess station.

I whisper to Mary Beth, "Do you recognize anyone at that table over there?" I motion for her to look under the table and point in their direction.

Mary Beth looks down at my hand and then at the other table. "Oh, crap. Those are the union guys from the Concrete and Cement Union," she says. "Why do you think they are here?" she asks.

"There is no way they knew we would be here tonight," I say.

Our waiter comes over to our table with two bottles of red wine. "These bottles of red wine are from the four gentlemen over at table four," he says, looking back at the Union men.

We all glance toward table four and wave. Lizzy blows them a kiss. "Please thank them for us. This is very sweet, as this is our last night in New York," I say.

I already knew who sent it. The man who winked at me had been watching me since I walked in. I can't imagine this happening tonight.

"Mary Beth, we are going over to their table to thank them and chat. You are following my lead," I say.

"Got it," says Mary Beth.

"Lizzy, come over in a couple of minutes and bring your cell phone. I am going to convince those guys to get pictures with us. Get your camera ready and make sure you get pictures of their faces," I say.

Mary Beth and I walk over to table four. "Thank you, gentlemen, for the wine. This is our last night in New York, and you have made our evening special. I'm Sara, and this is Mary Beth," I say, smiling at the men.

The good-looking Italian grabs my hand, turns it palm up, and kisses my palm. "My name is Anthony, but my friends call me Tony," he says, looking deep into my eyes.

"Oh," I smile while my stomach is turning somersault.

Mary Beth moves between two of the other guys and places her hands on their shoulders.

"Tony, I notice you have on a pinky ring. Are you a labor union member?" I ask with a smile.

"Yes, how do you know this?" he asks, glaring at my eyes.

"My husband is a business agent for a local union in Tampa. I look at all the union magazines and notice some unions give pinky rings for years of service. I always thought that was a great idea. My husband's union gives the guys a gold union watch for their anniversaries. Of course, they are not real gold," I say.

"I see that you all are wearing pinky rings," says Mary Beth.

Lizzy comes over to the table with her camera and asks if she can take some pictures of us girls and the men. Mary Beth asks, "Please, can I sit on your lap if you don't mind?"

"Of course," says the man with the black mustache.

I grab my phone out of my pocket and snap off a couple of pictures as Mary Beth moves from man to man. I think she is enjoying this a little too much. Lizzy snaps pictures, too, and then Tony grabs me by the waist and asks, "Sara, how about you sit here with me, and let's get our picture taken?"

"Sure, Tony," I say, sitting on his lap. I hope I don't hurl.

"Can I get your cell number so I can send you guys copies of our pictures?" I ask sweetly.

Tony whispers in my ear, "Sara, give me your phone, and I will give you my private number. I travel a lot, and maybe you can join me on some of those trips. Our little secret," he adds, kissing my neck.

"You are a tease," I say, giving him a quick peck on the cheek. He gives me the creeps, and I can't wait to return to our table.

The waiter brings the men their meals, and the hostess brings another bottle of red wine to the table. This is our cue to hurry back to our table. "Got them all," whispers Lizzy.

"Great job, girls," I say to Mary Beth and Lizzy.

We drink our wine and nibble on the cheese and bread. The waiter is waiting for us to order. "I'm sorry we took so long," I say.

"No worries, ladies. That is Mr. Tony; he owns Carmine's. He has told me that whatever you want, you get, and it is on the house," exclaims the waiter.

I wave to the table and give Tony a wink and air kiss. After all, we get a free meal, and chances are he gets prison time.

I order the lasagna and Caesar salad. Lizzy orders the manicotti and Caesar salad. Mary Beth orders chicken parmesan. Cici and Nancy order spaghetti and meatballs with side salads, and Elle orders veal parmesan with fettuccine alfredo. "Make sure you add onions and extra olives to my salad. You know that onions are high in antioxidants," says Cici.

The men finish their meals and come over to our table. "Ladies, I hope you come back to New York soon," says Tony looking right at me.

"Thank you for a lovely night, dinner, and wine," I say.

"Wait!" yells Cici. "We want our pictures with you guys, too," she adds. Nancy jumps up and heads to the bathroom The men gather behind the other girls, and the waiter takes the picture.

Tony gives me a wink, and the men leave the restaurant.

I notice Nancy hanging back in the dark hallway to the restrooms. She doesn't come to the table until the men leave the building. "What's going on?" I ask. "I saw you waiting in the hallway until those men left," I add.

"The guy talking to you is known as Tony the Terror. He is suspected of drug dealing and even a couple of murders," whispers Nancy. "The government has had him under surveillance for a few years now," she adds.

"Thank God they are gone; Tony was creeping me out," I say.

After dinner, the waiter takes our plates back to the kitchen. He brings back a platter of different Italian desserts: cannolis, tiramisu, and Torta Settevelli. "Compliments of Mr. Tony," he says.

We eat the desserts; after all, they cost us nothing.

I call Andrew on my cell, "Andrew, we are ready to go back to the Plaza."

"I will be there in five minutes," he responds.

"Andrew is on his way to pick us up," I announce.

The limo arrives, and all the ladies gather inside.

"How was your dinner?" asks Andrew as he loads us into the limo.

Cici groans and falls into the side seat. Elle stretches out on the back seat, and the rest of us slide on the opposite seat from Cici.

"It was amazing," says Mary Beth. "I am so full. My momma would say that I am full as a pig."

Andrew laughs, closes the door, and drives us to the Plaza. He helps us out of the limo in front of the lobby. Before going in, I ask, "Andrew, we need to arrive at the airport at noon. Before we go to the airport, would you drive us to where they sell the knockoff purses? We want to check them out. What time should we meet you in the lobby?"

"Let's try to leave by ninety-thirty in the morning. That will give you ladies some time for shopping. It is a little rough down there, so you gals need to be careful. I will find a parking spot close by and keep an eye out for you. There will not be much traffic at that time on a Sunday morning," he says.

"Great, we will see you then; goodnight Andrew," I say and turn toward the elevator.

Once off the elevator, we make our way to the rooms, say goodnight, and then rush off to our beds. I have a hard time sleeping and get out of bed around two o'clock for some water. I hear sirens blaring from outside and immediately walk out onto the balcony. Apparently, a fight broke out down below as I see police officers pulling a man into a cop car and two other men in the street holding a police officer and yelling something. It sounds like, "Get his gun! Get his gun!" Out of the corner of my eye, I see two other policemen come from a dark alley behind the two guys with the cop. The police have their weapons out and rush the other men. In a matter of seconds, the two bad guys are on the ground, and the police officers are handcuffing them. I look over and see Lizzy, Elle, and Cici clapping like they are watching a movie. People on the streets and other hotel balconies join in, and one of the cops removes his hat and bows. This could only happen in New York City, New York's finest in action.

I grab my water bottle and head back to bed.

Chapter Thirty-Seven

I wake up at eight o'clock the next morning, all excited to be going home to see Weston. I haven't seen him in almost a week; I miss my man. My brain is also overloaded due to all that has happened. I need to get home to think. I pour myself a cup of black coffee and walk outside onto the balcony to see what's happening in Times Square this morning. All is quiet on the square. It will not get busy until around ten o'clock when the stores and box office tickets open. The air is chilly, and the temperature is around forty degrees. Lizzy is wrapped up in a thick, blue blanket and is already up and sitting on her balcony.

"Good morning," I say, stretching my arms over my head.

"Good morning, Sara. Did you sleep well last night?" she asks.

"I slept like a big tree log lying in a gator swamp. After the excitement from last night, I could barely keep my eyes open." I say. "How about you?" I ask.

"I really slept hard after the sirens stopped. I was so tired when we left Carmine's that I could barely hold my head up in the limo," says Lizzy taking a sip of her coffee mixed with a little honey.

"It was a great night, even with all the noise," I add.

"I will be glad when we turn over our case file to Agent Watts," Lizzy says. "Last night was a bit scary," she adds.

"I will be glad to clear this mess up too. This whole investigation is getting way too much for us to handle on our own. Did you see the look on Nancy's face when Tony and the other guys came toward our table?" I asked.

"Yes, she was really frightened," says Lizzy. "Did you see her standing in the bathroom hallway waiting for the men to leave?" she asks.

"Yes, I spoke with her about that," I say. "Next weekend, Weston is going on a fishing trip. He leaves on Wednesday afternoon and returns Saturday night. I am going to ask all the Beach Girls to come to my house for lunch. I will make sure our file on Sonny is updated and will get the pictures developed. We can inform them about the case and discuss our next step," I say.

"Sara, you know Cici is not going to be happy that we did not tell them this weekend," says Lizzy.

"I know, but they will have to get past that. Right now, my focus is on keeping us all safe and getting out of this town," I state.

"But look what happened at Carmine's last night," she says.

"Lizzy, that was last night, and they all think it was a fun night. I don't want to ruin that for anyone. We are safe and will turn the case over to the feds after we get home and update the girls," I say.

Nancy and Cici come out onto the balcony wrapped in their blue blankets.

"Good morning, ladies," I say.

"Good morning, my lovely friends. I decided to go home this morning so you guys can get ready to fly home," says Nancy. "This weekend has been a blast, and I can't thank you enough, Sara," she adds.

"You can't go this morning. We are going to buy some knockoff handbags. You have to be with us, or it won't be as much fun," I say. "I know you have a couple of knockoffs yourself," I add.

"Don't you want to see us off to the airport?" I ask with sad eyes and a droopy, doggie face. "I will get Andrew to take you home afterward," I add.

"Well, since you look so sad with your puppy dog face, how can I not," says Nancy with a quick wink. "By the way, the knockoff purses are just a New York thing. I have nothing to do with any of that," she adds.

All the Beach Girls meet in the dining room on our floor for breakfast. I have soft, scrambled eggs, bacon, and whole wheat toast with habanero and blackberry jelly. I love the spicy, sweet taste of the jelly on my toast.

Cici, Nancy, and Elle get the New York bagels and fruit. Lizzy and Mary Beth have sausage links, eggs, and fruit.

"Last night's show music was incredible. I keep hearing Sherry Baby in my head," says Lizzy.

"I loved the Jersey Boys, and those guys were unbelievable. They sounded just like the original," says Mary Beth.

"I still can't believe the guys took pictures with us and let us go backstage. I felt like a celebrity," says Cici.

"Oh, speaking of pictures, will you all please send me the pictures from Carmine's last night? I want to add a few to my vacation book," I say. Whenever I take a big vacation, I create a photo book with pictures and sayings. Our New York trip will be no exception. "I also need the pictures of Tony and his men for our file on Sonny Manuzco," I continue, knowing I will not mention the real truth at this time.

Mathew hurries to our table, "Good morning, ladies. I hope you enjoyed your stay with us and hope you will visit again soon," he says.

"Mathew, come take a picture with us," I say as the ladies gather up from their seats and reach for their cameras. A nice gentleman sitting at a table next to ours gets up and says, "Ladies, I will be glad to take your pictures."

"Thank you," I say and hand him my phone first.

Lizzy hands the nice man her phone next and on and on with the picture taking.

"You are very sweet to take all of those pictures," says Mary Beth as she hands me her phone. "Sara, take a picture of this kind gentleman and me," she adds.

Here we go again. By the time we finished taking the pictures, Mary Beth knows the man's name and cell phone number. I hand Mathew a small envelope with two hundred dollar bills inside.

"Thank you, Mathew, for being so nice to us. We will miss you," I say.

"Bye!" yell all the girls as we step into the elevator. Mary Beth gives Mathew a peck on the cheek, and he pushes the button to the lobby. Down we go.

Our luggage has been sent ahead for Andrew to load into the limo. I walk up to the hotel check out, hand them my card and head out to the limo with the other ladies.

"Good morning, ladies," says Andrew. "Did you sleep well after your night of partying?" he asks.

"Yes, we had a great time," I say, handing Andrew a small envelope with three one-hundred-dollar bills. After all, he chauffeured us around the city for three days and nights. The big tip is well deserved.

After we get into the limo, I ask, "Andrew, after you take us shopping and to the airport, will you drop Nancy off at her apartment in Chelsea?"

"I would be happy to, Mrs. Springs," he replies.

Andrew drops us at the corner of Houston and State Streets. We hustle out of the limo and gather on the sidewalk. A few feet ahead, we hear people haggling with the store owners. We walk up to a makeshift building, and a lady motions for us to come in. It looks a little scary, so we all squeeze in together. Handbags are hanging everywhere. We look around inside the small cubicle for a few minutes, and then the lady says, "If you want to get the best handbags, you need to come into the back room. I can only take two of you ladies at a time. You must pay cash."

Lizzy and I go first. When we walk into the small room, the lady closes the door behind us. I must say, we get a little frightened; however, when I see a red Gucci bag, I know I had to have it. I grab the bag, pay the woman cash and exit out the door, leaving Lizzy behind. I grab Mary Beth by the arm and push her into the room. A couple of minutes later, Lizzy and Mary Beth come out the door, holding a plastic bag full of purses.

"I bought my girls some bags for their birthdays," says Mary Beth.

Nancy refuses to go into the back room, but Cici and Elle have no fear. It only took a few minutes for them to come out with their knockoff bags. We are all very happy with our counterfeit purses; after all, that is one of the things New York is known for. Now, how are we getting them home?

As we walk down the street, looking at all the small shops, we hear a siren and see women and men running down the street with huge plastic bags of purses. One man trips and loses two Gucci bags. The counterfeit bags go flying into the middle of Houston Street, right in the middle of traffic. Mary Beth looks at the bags, and I grab her arm.

"Leave them alone. You are not going into the middle of the street," I whisper into her ear.

"I can get them," she replies, trying to get away from me.

"Not today, sister," I say, holding firmly to her arm. Someone has to watch out for that woman, and I guess today is my turn.

I glance down the street and locate Andrew standing and waving next to the limo. I hustle the girls with their bags to the limo and out of the hectic environment.

"Hurry, ladies, Andrew is just down the street," I yell.

Once we get into the limo, I say, "To the airport, Andrew, before we end up in the New York City jail."

"Yes, ma'am," Andrew responds, and off we go.

Once we arrive at the departure terminal, Andrew checks our baggage for us. We all give Nancy a goodbye hug.

"See you at the Sea Glass Beach House," I say, waving goodbye.

"Bye, everybody!" yells Nancy.

We walk into the airport and make our way to the security lines. I look down and see Cici walking behind me. "What have you got on your feet?!" I yell.

"What? I thought they looked cool," she says, looking down at her boots.

"Cici, you have to take your shoes off. What were you thinking wearing knee-high, lace-up, leather boots to an airport?" I ask, feeling stressed; we can't miss our flight.

The other ladies have their hands on their mouths, covering their snickering as they continue to the checkpoint. Cici is not going to live this down any time soon.

"Oh crap," says Cici as she walks over to the nearest bench to remove her boots.

"Everybody else, please get into line. I will stay with Cici while she takes her boots off," I say.

"I will save you two a spot in line, so hurry up. It looks like the line is moving pretty fast," says Lizzy.

Fifteen minutes later, Cici removes her boots.

"You don't have socks on?" I ask. "Never mind," I say, reaching in my carry-on bag for a pair of socks. I keep a pair in there in case my feet get cold while I am traveling. I grab a pair of bright red socks and hand them to Cici. "Here, put these on," I say.

I look up for the girls, and they are almost at the security desk. I grab Cici and slide her in the red socks to the front of the line where Mary Beth is frantically waving her hands back and forth and yelling. "Hurry up!"

"Whew, we made it," I say once we are in line.

Elle is laughing so hard; the people in the lines next to us are laughing too. Cici is waving to everybody like she is on a parade float.

We make it through security. I say, "Cici, you are not putting on your boots until we are on the airplane."

"Fine, I will just look like a tall Christmas elf," says Cici laughing and waving to all the passengers. I love her free spirit.

We arrive at our departure gate just as the steward announces, "We will begin loading seats one through eight at this time."

Lizzy and I sit in seats one and two, with my seat near the window. Cici and Elle sit in seats three and four, with Cici in the aisle seat. Mary Beth is in seat five, which just happens to be next to a good-looking, thirtysomething male wearing jeans, cowboy boots, and a denim shirt. She looks up at me, gives me a wink, and smiles at the man.

The stewardess announces the safety rules, the plane takes off, and I fall asleep. I sleep for almost an hour. Lizzy gives me a little shake, saying, "Hey, girl, it's time for lunch. Do you want the chicken wrap or the cheese and fruit tray?"

"Cheese and fruit is fine. I am still full from breakfast," I say.

Lunch arrives; the cheese and fruit is quite tasty. I glance back at Mary Beth, and she is giggling. Her seat partner is keeping her entertained. Cici and Elle have ordered the chicken wraps and appear to be enjoying their food. Both of them have glasses of wine. I wish I had ordered a glass.

We arrive at JAX and immediately exit the airplane. Having first-class tickets is worth the money. We head down the escalator to the baggage claim area. Weston is standing next to the luggage carousel, waiting for me. I walk quickly up to him and kiss him on the lips.

"I missed you," I say.

"I missed you, too," says Weston. "How was the trip? Did the girls behave?" he asks.

"Pretty much. We had a great time and a lot of fun. You won't believe what happened," I say.

While waiting for our luggage, we all hug and say goodbye. The Beach Girls hug Weston too.

"Don't forget lunch at my house next Saturday," I say.

"What can I bring?" asks Elle.

"I am making chili, so if you want to bring some crackers, that will work," I respond.

"What do you want me to bring?" asks Mary Beth.

"Nothing, a few crackers is all we need. I have everything else," I answer.

Weston picks up my luggage, and we head to the short-term parking lot.

"Did you find out anything new about Sonny's life?" he asks.

"Weston, you are not going to believe everything that happened," I say. "You were right about the union connection with Sonny's ring," I add.

We walk to our Chevy SUV, and Weston places the luggage into the back. He closes the trunk door and gets in the driver's gray leather seat. "Now, tell me what actually happened in New York," he says.

"Well, Sonny worked for the Local 123 Concrete and Cement Union. He lived with his mother in New York's Little Italy. She hasn't seen him since he left to work in Florida. Mary Beth and I stopped into the Union Hall for a look and saw several photos of Sonny and some other men. I think we could have the connection to his murder," I say.

I didn't tell him everything because I didn't want to worry Weston any more.

Chapter Thirty-Eight

The next week was a noneventful week at school. On Tuesday, Weston and I attended our grandson Rylan's football game at his middle school. He scored two touchdowns, and his team won by twenty points. Wednesday, we watched Caroline riding her horse, English style. She looked amazing on top of her chestnut mare with the black mane. On Thursday, we went to Brooks' junior varsity football game. He played linebacker and was fierce. He made four solo tackles and recovered a fumble. The Beach Girls love their grandchildren, and if there is a sports event, school play, band practice, or 4H pig showing, we are there. Mary Beth's granddaughter, Faith, has a show pig, "Dolly Porkin."

Saturday morning arrives, and I set out to make lunch. The chili was cooking all day Friday, so I only had to heat it in the crockpot. As it heats, the aroma permeates the entire house; it is wonderful. For dessert, I pull a large bowl from the kitchen cabinet and grab the cream cheese and heavy whipping cream from the refrigerator. I place the heavy whipping cream into the bowl and use my mixer to make it fluffy. Then, I add the softened cream cheese and blend the mixture. I get my ladyfingers and line a trifle bowl along the bottom and sides. Next, I fill the trifle half full with the cream cheese mixture and place fresh strawberries on top. My last layer is the cream mixture with blueberries. The dessert is complete. I place the trifle into the refrigerator for cooling.

The Beach Girls arrive at twelve; I have lunch prepared: chili, crescent rolls, sweet "assed" tea for Cici, and the fresh fruit trifle. Elle has the crackers in a dish and sets them on the kitchen island along with the other food.

"This looks great!" exclaims Elle.

"Yes, and I love how you decorate for the seasons," says Lizzy.

"Well, spring starts next week, and I can't wait for all the flowers to bloom and the little bunnies to come out of their holes. We have about six wild rabbits and would have had more if the hawks didn't get them," I say. "Thanks, Elle, for picking up the crackers for me. I had everything else," I add.

"I planted my little garden this morning. I was up at six; you know I am an early-morning person. I planted my herbs, onions, and carrots and washed the car before coming over," says Cici. "You know I take those natural vitamins and have so much energy now," adds Cici staring at me with her eyes wide open.

"You can come to my house and plant some flowers if you have so much energy," says Mary Beth. "But, if you want them to bloom, you had better plant the silk ones," she adds, laughing.

"Yeah, Mary Beth doesn't water anything around her house. Do you ever go out into your yard?" asks Lizzy.

"I only go out to get in the car. I have people mow the grass and trim the trees and stuff," says Mary Beth. "My yard always looks manicured," she says, wiggling her nose.

We fill our plates and open a bottle of wine. After lunch, the ladies clear the table and clean the kitchen while I walk to my office and retrieve Sonny's case file. I set the timeline on my tripod and lay the pictures in time order across the table. The ladies return to the dining room table and take a seat.

"Ladies, I need to update everyone on our case," I say. "There has been a lot of information revealed since we last spoke about Sonny. Weston, my dad, and I took our trip to Biloxi," I say.

"We know that. That is where you won all that money," says Elle.

"Yes, but what you don't know is that I recognized Sonny's picture in one of the casinos. His name is Sonny Manuzco. He lived in New York City," I say. "He was a big winner at the casino and had his picture placed on the wall of the Winner's Circle," I add.

"Is that why you and Mary Beth went to New York earlier than us?" asks Elle.

"Yes, Mary Beth has a friend at the post office who transferred a year ago from New York. He was able to contact some friends and get the address for us. Mary Beth did not tell him why she needed the address since we didn't want anyone else involved. He lived in Little Italy with his mother," I say.

"I searched around the house while Sara was speaking to his mother. There were some weird things going on around there," says Mary Beth.

"What kind of weird stuff?" asks Cici.

"Well, they have a very unusual satellite in the backyard; the regular TV dish is on the roof of the house. There was a new in-ground pool back there too. I also saw a new Cadillac SUV and a new Dodge truck with those fancy wheels," says Mary Beth.

"I can't imagine any concrete or cement union guy having that kind of money unless something is going on," says Lizzy.

"After we left his house, we ate at a nearby Italian family restaurant. We met a waitress, and I asked her if she knew Sonny. She told us that he was mean to the kids in the neighborhood," I say.

"Wait one minute," says Cici. "Did he ever hurt any of those kids?" she asks.

"I don't know about that, but she told us he worked for the Concrete and Cement Union a few blocks away. Mary Beth and I visited the union hall. The receptionist was a beautiful, Italian young woman who gave us a little tour around the building," I say. "Of course, it helped that we used our southern charm while we were with her."

"Yes, she showed us into the conference hall, and there were pictures of Sonny and some other union guys. We told her we were from Tampa and that Sara's husband was a local union guy," says Mary Beth.

"The pictures of the guys from the union hall are of the same men who paid for our dinner at Carmine's. Tony is the local president and has a very bad reputation," I say.

"So that's why you girls were flirting and wanting to take pictures," says Elle.

"Yes, I recognized their pinkie rings when I walked past their table. Tony was staring holes through me, as I smiled at him. He winked, and I knew we had to get those pictures. He is a real creep," I say.

"Yeah, but he is handsome and paid for our dinners," says Mary Beth.

"When I got to our table, I told Mary Beth to come with me and follow my lead. By that time, she, too, recognized the men. I also asked Lizzy to come over a couple of minutes later to take some pictures," I say.

"I thought they were all creeps. That one fat dude couldn't keep his hands off of Mary Beth," says Lizzy.

"He wasn't so bad," says Mary Beth.

"Let me get this straight. You three knew the whole time and didn't think about telling us?" asks Cici.

"That's right. Lizzy and Mary Beth already knew too much. I didn't want anyone to get hurt. The reason for the trip was to have fun, not to get anyone harmed. On Wednesday, Mary Beth and I rented a Chevy Equinox and drove to Sonny's neighborhood. Both of us dressed as businesswomen, wearing pantsuits and tailored shirts. You should have seen us dressed as professional women. We never intended to go to the house, but I couldn't help myself. As soon as I knocked on the door, Mary Beth took off around the side of the house. I told his mother that I was from the transportation authority in Florida and needed to speak to Sonny Manuzco. That's when she said Sonny was in Florida working and staying with his friend Franks. It did not occur to me until later the connection between Detective Franks and Sonny," I say.

"We were followed the next day when we went shopping in Chelsea," says Mary Beth.

"What!?" yells Cici staring right into my eyes.

"We bought stun guns when we arrived; we know how to watch our backs," says Mary Beth. "We must have walked that man to death because, after lunch, we did not see him again," she adds.

"I guess he didn't figure we were much of a threat since he quit following us after we picked you guys up at the airport. Andrew noticed him following the limo and told me at the airport when I got out. I asked him to keep an eye out," I say.

"What's our next move?" asks Cici.

"I am going to call Agent Watts, Nancy's friend, and turn over all of our research. I think we should set a meeting with her next Saturday; we should all be there," I say.

"I think we should meet out at the farm in MacClenny. After the meeting, y'all can stay for lunch. Please don't bring anything," says Lizzy.

"How about a couple of bottles of Moscato?" asks Elle.

"Sure, we can always use wine," says Lizzy.

"Is everybody available for next Saturday? We can meet at Lizzy's at eleven and get the meeting over by twelve or twelve-thirty," I say.

"Yes," they all say in unison.

"Please watch your backs this week and don't talk to anyone, including each other. Nothing over the phone," I say. "This is dangerous business," I add.

"Did any of you tell those men at Carmine's where we are from?" I ask.

"I didn't," says Lizzy.

"I heard you say Tampa, and I went along with that," says Mary Beth.

"I didn't," says Cici.

"Me either, and I know that Nancy didn't because she left the table to go to the restroom," says Elle.

"Why did she leave the table in such a hurry?" asks Elle.

"She recognized the men as belonging to the drug cartel. The DEA agents are investigating their union; she didn't want to be seen around them," I say.

"Understandable," says Elle.

"Okay, we should be ready for our meeting," I say.

On Sunday, I call Nancy.

"Hello," Nancy answers.

"Hi Nancy, how are you and the family?" I ask.

"We are all doing fine. How about you?" she asks.

"Everyone is fine. Nancy, I need to fill you in on the Sea Glass House murder case," I say.

"Ok, I agree it is time you do, especially after our dinner with the mob at Carmine's," she says.

"The deceased's name is Sonny Manuzco, and he was a union boss for New York's Concrete and Cement Union. He has a house in Little Italy, and his mother lives with him Mary Beth and I met her. She told us that Sonny was working in Florida and was staying with a friend named Franks," I say.

"I knew I didn't like that man the first time I saw him at the Sea Glass House," says Nancy.

"I am going to set up a meeting with Agent Watts for next weekend with the other Beach Girls. The meeting will be at eleven o'clock at Lizzy's farmhouse. I am also making a copy of our file for you and will mail it overnight on Friday. You should get it Saturday morning," I say.

"I don't want you and the other girls doing any more investigating. Let Rachel handle everything from here," says Nancy firmly.

"We will; I promise," I say. "How is the new granddaughter?" I ask.

"She is an angel and is just starting the cooing sounds," says Nancy.

"If she is anything like her grandmother, she must be a little angel," I say.

We talk for a few more minutes until I hear Weston calling me.

"I've got to go, Nancy. We will speak next weekend," I say.

"Sara! These red snappers will be ready in a few minutes. Have you made the salad?" Weston asks. He came home this morning with a cooler full of red snapper and is grilling them on the gas grill out by the pool.

Today, I am spending my time with Weston. We will eat the fish he caught, drink wine, and relax. I am glad to be home.

Chapter Thirty-Nine

I call Agent Watts on Monday morning.

"Agent Watts, this is Sara Springs. I think we need to meet. Is it possible for you to meet the Beach Girls out at Lizzy's farmhouse this Saturday at eleven?" I say.

"Yes, I can meet you there. What is going on?" she asks.

"I can't talk about it over the phone. I will explain everything on Saturday," I say

It was an uneventful week at the school. However, Weston and I got to spend time with our grandchildren and their parents. They have the best parents, of course, and the best grandparents. On Tuesday, our grandson, Rylan, played baseball with his travel team. He is a left-handed pitcher and runs like a deer. When he gets on base, you know he is already thinking about getting to home plate. He scored two runs and went two for three at bat.

Wednesday, I got a call from my granddaughter, Caroline. "Hey, Nana, I need to ask you a question," she said.

"Okay, sweet pea. What is it?" I responded.

"Is 'was' a being verb? I am in the car on my way to a football banquet, doing my homework," Caroline said.

Not surprised, I responded, "Yes, it is."

"Nana, are you sure?" she asked.

I looked it up on Weston's iPhone and replied, "I looked it up on Google, and there is a list: is, are, were, was, and more. I will take a screenshot and text it to you. Whose phone are you using?" I asked.

"I have Momma's, so you can send it to her. I love you, Nana," she said. That child looks just like her daddy and is just as smart.

Thursday, we went to Brooks' junior varsity baseball game. He is extremely strong and hits the ball hard. Brooks is fast, too, and plays left field. Brooks hit two doubles off the fence and walked once. His team won the game seven to five.

Saturday morning, I get up early and meet Weston by the pool with a cup of coffee. Saturday is our morning to spend some time discussing the previous week. We sit by the pool, drinking our coffee and enjoying the morning.

"Today is the day you hand over your casework to the feds, right?" asks Weston.

"Yes. I need to let you in on something else, though," I say.

"Go ahead; what is it?" he asks and then takes a sip of his coffee.

"I don't know if I can teach anymore. Yesterday, one of my students, Travis, was arrested in class for attempted murder. The detectives came right into the classroom with the principal, grabbed his arms, and led him out of the room. Supposedly, Travis went over to his girlfriend's house on Thursday, and they planned to kill her ex-boyfriend. The kids say she called the ex-boyfriend and asked him to come to her house. Travis was hiding behind a bush, and when the guy got out of the car, Travis fired his shotgun. The only thing that saved the boy was that Travis had buckshot in his gun. This is the second time this year one of my students has been arrested. Early this year, one was arrested for sexual assault on a child under ten. I feel so bad. I know these kids have bad lives, but come on," I say.

"Well, baby, you can't win them all. I know you do everything you can to help them; you are not their parents. Maybe it is time to leave teaching. I hate seeing you work so hard," says Weston taking my hand in his.

I look at my cell phone; it is already nine o'clock.

"I have to get dressed and get over to Lizzy's," I say to Weston.

"You, girls, watch out and be careful. Once you give the information to the feds, stop investigating," says Weston. "You make me worry too much," he adds.

I dress in jeans and a blue pullover sweater, pick up Sonny's case file and head out to the garage for my car. "I have got to keep these ladies safe, turn the file over to Agent Watts, and get back to my so-called normal life," I murmur.

Chapter Forty

My drive to Lizzy's beautiful farmhouse is relaxing. The scenery is tall blue skies, green pine trees, and large fields of spring flowers. The sun is shining, and the birds, red cardinals, blue jays, and white cowbirds, are flying across the baby blue sky. My mood is changing, and that is a good thing.

I pull off the gravel road onto Honeydew Lane. The lane is made of red clay and leads directly to Lizzy's wood and stone house. A stacked stone entranceway with a gray gate opens into the drive, and I move my SUV forward to park. The house has a large, green field with cattle on one side about a hundred feet from the house. Behind the house is a large open, red barn with a small chicken house nearby. As I open the door to my SUV, I hear the rooster crowing. On the other side of the house is another large, green field with more cattle. The only way in and out of the farm is by the Honeydew roadway.

I get out of my SUV and go up on the porch. Lizzy answers the double doors.

"Hello, Sara. Come on in; I'm working in the kitchen," she says and leads me into the kitchen.

"Thanks. Do you need some help?" I ask as I place the file on the table.

"No. I closed the garage door and the small entrance door to the garage. I also lowered the blinds in all the rooms. I've been checking the road out of the kitchen window every few minutes. I don't want any surprises. You know the feds; they could have a dozen agents out there in the woods," says Lizzy.

"We are just having a meeting with Agent Watts," I say. "I don't think anything will happen today," I add hopefully.

At that moment, I look out the window and see Cici, Elle, and Mary Beth driving down the dirt road and watch as they pull into Lizzy's front drive. Lizzy heads to the front door, opens it, and says, "Hey y'all; come on in. Sara is already in the kitchen."

I stand in the kitchen looking out the window again and see Agent Watts' black SUV make a turn onto Honeydew Lane. She is just reaching the dirt road when I see a Chevy Silverado truck slowly turn onto Honeydew. Agent Watts parks in front of the farmhouse, and Lizzy opens the door to let her in.

I keep watching the truck. At first, I think they are going to turn around because the truck slows down. Then, two men open the doors and step out onto the road. One man has camouflage clothing on and the other is wearing dress pants, a shirt, and a jacket. They both look familiar, but I can't identify them. The men pull out pistols and hide the guns beneath their jackets. I look back at the Beach Girls and shout, "We have two men with guns heading our way!"

Agent Watts comes over to the window and grabs her gun from her holster. Mary Beth and Elle run for their purses and pull out their guns. Mary Beth's gun is pink, and Elle has a blue one. Elle grabs her pistol while Cici hinds behind her. I grab the cast iron frying pan off the stovetop.

"Cici and Elle get into the safe room in my bedroom closet. Elle, lock the door and call the cops," says Lizzy.

Elle dials 911, "Hello, we are at 54628 Honeydew Lane in MacClenny. There are two intruders trying to break into the house. They are both armed with weapons. Agent Watts with the FBI is with us."

"Are there any children with you? How many men and women?" asks the 911 operator.

"There are five women, no children and no men with us. Call the FBI and the county cops and tell them to hurry," states Cici yelling into Elle's phone.

"All of you get into that safe room!" screams Watts.

"Not on your life," says Lizzy reaching for the drawer next to her wooden sink and pulling out her gun. "We are protecting our friends and my house," she adds.

"We know how to shoot a gun," yells Mary Beth.

"Yeah, and I know how to swing a frying pan," I say. "After all, I played softball for years and am a pretty good athlete."

"They are splitting up; one is coming around the back, and the other man in the suit is heading toward the front door," I whisper.

"Okay, you ladies take the backdoor. I will go out through the garage and take the man in front," says Agent Watts.

"Lizzy and Mary Beth, get behind the door next to the wall," I say. "I am going to hit him with the frying pan and try to knock his gun away as he comes through. You two aim your guns at his head and don't miss if he tries to shoot," I add.

Agent Watts moves quickly through the garage, locks the small door, and hustles toward the thick green shrubs. The bushes are just large enough to hide her tall frame as she moves swiftly behind the bushes toward the front door. The agent points her pistol toward the man as she makes her way down the long side of the house to the front porch.

Standing next to the wall beside the backdoor, I hear the man pushing a knife into the lock, trying to open the door. He holds his weapon in his right arm and pushes on the door. The door slowly inches open, and I see the gun. I raise my frying pan and swing downward hard enough to crack his bones. The gun goes flying into the kitchen. I raise my cast iron frying pan again and bring it down on the man's head. Lizzy is there with her gun aimed next to the man's head while Mary Beth is aiming at his private parts.

"Did I kill him?" I ask, putting the frying pan on the kitchen counter.

"Oh no, that is James Kilroy," says Lizzy.

Back in the safe room, Cici starts to cry. "Please, Elle, we have got to get out of here and help them. Please, please let me out," she says.

"Cici, we were told to stay in here until they came to get us," says Elle.

"When have we ever obeyed anyone? Get that door open. Now!" yells Cici.

"Okay, but you get behind me. I have the gun!" screams Elle. The two move cautiously down the hallway to the kitchen entrance. "You don't have to lie on my back," whispers Elle using her left hand to push Cici back. Her right hand with the blue pistol is aimed straight ahead.

In the kitchen, I kneel down next to the man to check his pulse and see blood oozing down the back of his head. Lizzy, with her gun still pointed at the man's head, reaches inside one of the cabinet drawers, and takes out a dishcloth. She hands it to me.

"No, not this one. It is one of my good towels," says Lizzy. She reaches back into the drawer and picks up a dishcloth stained with grease. "Here, take this one," she says.

I place the towel on the man's head and grab his wrist to feel his pulse. He is still alive. "Lizzy, do you have any duct tape?" I ask. "We can tape his legs and wrists together before he wakes up. Mary Beth, you keep the gun on him in case he wakes up before we have him taped," I add.

"Yes, over here in another drawer," she says, reaching for the metallic red roll of duct tape. She hands it to me just as the man wakes up.

"That is the man from the Octagon house! I'd know that creep anywhere," yells Elle. I turn my head slightly and see Elle and Cici entering the room.

"We told you two to stay in the safe room," says Lizzy.

"Let me in here," says Cici, pushing me away and kneeling by the man. "She slaps the man's face twice. "How dare you kill another human, you monster! Give me that duct tape," she shouts, hitting the Octagon house man again.

"Here it is," I say, handing over the tape. Cici snatches a piece of tape and tightly wraps his ankles and wrists together.

"You ladies do remember that I am a nurse," says Cici.

"What are you bitches doing to me?" asks the Octagon man.

"I don't want to hear another word out of you, stupid," says Cici. She snatches another piece of tape and whispers to the animal, "You think you are a stud, don't you, with your shirt open? Well, let's see what kind of stud you are when the cops rip this tape off your bony chest," she adds sticking a wide piece of red metallic duct tape across his hairy chest.

Bang! Bang!

"Oh my God, Mary Beth and Elle bring the guns. That must have been Agent Watts."

We run to the front door and peek out the side door window. Agent Watts has the suited man on the ground, placing her handcuffs on his wrists. I see blood coming out of his white shirt right at his shoulder. I open the door and step out.

"That's Detective Franks!" I yell. "You piece of crap," I add, kicking him in his side.

"It's you! You b...," he starts to say, but Agent Watts kicks him in the groin.

"Good shot," I say.

"Are you ladies alright?" Agent Watts asks.

"Yes, the other one is in the kitchen. We taped him up in duct tape. He has a cut on his head from the frying pan," I say.

"Yeah, Cici and Lizzy have him on the floor," says Mary Beth.

"I thought we told Elle and Cici to stay in the safe room? Never mind," says Watts.

Sirens blare, and red and blue lights rush our way. It looks like every cop car in the county is on the road. Three black SUVs pull up in the yard, and ten agents come running.

"Throw your guns down," yell the men.

Mary Beth and Elle immediately throw their guns down in the grass, and the three of us move closer together. The feds surround the farmhouse with guns ready to fire.

Agent Watts pulls her badge from her pocket and screams, "FBI Agent Watts, put your guns away. The intruders have been captured; we need a couple of ambulances here right away."

"Okay, okay," says Agent Anderson. "Matt, call for the ambulances, and you two go inside," he adds.

The two agents enter the kitchen and ask Lizzy to put her gun on the kitchen island. She places the gun on the island, but Cici stays beside the Octagon House man.

"Ma'am, you can get up now. We will take it from here," says one of the agents.

"I would, but this jerk might try to move, and if he does, I will smack him right across his face. He killed a man," says Cici.

The cop moves next to Cici, "Ma'am, if he moves, I will kick him in the crotch," he says, giving Cici a hand up.

"I am Agent Jones and this is Agent Page. What happened here," he asks.

"Well, he broke into my house to kill us, and Sara hit him with my cast iron frying pan. It knocked him out, and then, we taped his arms and legs together," says Lizzy.

"And I put the tape on him. He killed that man at Matanzas Inlet," says Cici.

"Good work, ladies. I am impressed with your work," says Agent Jones.

"A crime scene unit is on its way," says Agent Page. "Let's get you, ladies, into the living area where you can relax a little," he adds.

Mary Beth, Elle, and I are led inside the living room, where Cici and Lizzy are sitting on the sofa.

"Please stay in here until the Crime Scene Unit has finished their work in the kitchen and outside around the house," says Agent Watts.

"Is it okay if I get us something to drink from the refrigerator in the garage?" asks Lizzy.

"Sure, just stay away from the kitchen," says Rachel.

An hour later, Agent Watts returns to the living room. "You did great today. The agents will be here shortly to ask you some more questions.

Please do not tell them about the file just yet. I need to investigate how Franks found out I was coming out here," says the agent. "You ladies did great today. I am so sorry things got a bit out of control, and you were put in harm's way," she adds as she leaves the room

"I hope this is the end of Sonny's murder," I say, laying my head back on the beige sofa and exhaling.

"Me too," adds Elle as she stretches her legs.

"That was great, Sara. When you hit Octagon's arm, I heard something snap. I hope you broke that creep's arm," says Mary Beth.

"Mary Beth, why were you pointing your pistol at his groin?" asks Lizzy.

"Would you move if a gun was pointed at your hoo-ha?" replies Mary Beth.

The other girls start laughing, and I know we will be fine.

"Lizzy, I am so sorry about the damage to your back door and the blood on the floor," I say.

"Don't worry about it. The Crime Scene technicians have some chemicals they are going to spray on the floor to clean up the mess. As far as the door is concerned, I already texted my neighbor, Kenny, and he is coming over later this evening to put a new lock on the door. I can paint the scratches next week," says Lizzy.

I look out the living room window and see the feds and paramedics load the two men into separate ambulances. I see the red metallic tape lying on the ground. I giggle when I notice a couple of pieces with a lot of hair sticking to them. "Cici, come look at this," I say.

"Ah ha, ha, ha, look at all that hair. I bet that really hurt," says Cici.

The other girls run over to the window and take a look. "Dang, Cici, it looks like a furry animal lying in the yard," says Elle.

"You know those men had a good time ripping that tape of the murderer," says Cici with a grin.

Agent Watts walks back into the living area and says, "The two intruders are being taken to the hospital and then to the federal lockup in Jacksonville. It is going to be a long time before they get out of prison. Agent Page is coming in now to ask you some questions."

Agent Page is a tall, black officer with a brilliant white smile. "Ladies, I have just a few questions, as Agent Watts has filled us in," he says. "Lizzy, this is your home, correct?" the agent asks.

"Yes, I have lived here for the last fifteen years," says Lizzy.

"I understand that you saw the men get out of that silver truck down the road a little way, Sara?" he asks.

"Yes, I was watching out of the kitchen window when I saw the truck pull onto the road just after Agent Watts arrived," I reply. "I saw the men hide their guns inside their jackets and split up. One went to the back, and the other went to the front yard," I add.

"Sara, what happened after that?" asks the agent.

"Lizzy and Mary Beth hid on one side, and I hid on the other side of the backdoor. When the man broke in, I hit him with the frying pan and knocked the gun from his hand, and then I hit him again on the head. Lizzy and Mary Beth had guns and immediately aimed their weapons at the man. I checked for a pulse and put a dishcloth on his wound. That's when Cici came in," I say.

"Cici, what happened after that?" Agent Reynolds asks.

"I kneeled beside him and checked his pulse again. Then I took the duct tape and wrapped his hands and feet. He woke up and called me a name, so I slapped him a few times. Lizzy put some duct tape on his mouth to shut him up. I tried to put another piece over his mouth, and he moved. The tape went onto his chest. I got another piece of tape and added it to his mouth," says Cici.

"Are we finished?" asks Elle. "It has been a long day, and I want to go home," she adds.

"Yes, we are done here. Thank you, ladies, and I am glad you handled yourself so well," says the agent as he stands and goes back into the kitchen.

Agent Watts returns, "Okay, the cops and CSI are done here and are heading back to the police station. I think the six of us need to have a little talk," she says.

"Yes, we have some pictures and notes for you," I say.

We walk into the dining room and sit around the table. I grab the file and place the timeline on my tripod while Lizzy lays the pictures out on the table.

"The man in the middle is Sonny Manuzco, the murder victim at the Sea Glass House. When my dad, Weston, and I went to Biloxi, I saw his picture on the wall in one of the casinos. I recognized his face and his pinky ring. My husband recognized the ring as one that the unions up north give as work anniversary gifts. Sonny is from New York City and works for the local Concrete and Cement Union. The man at the backdoor is the Octagon House man who killed Sonny. This is a picture of him coming from the house at Matanzas. The pictures of the other men are Sonny's union partners. We saw them at Carmine's on our last night in New York. I recognized the men as I walked by their table. I had seen a photograph of the men on the wall of the Union office conference hall when Mary Beth and I visited. We also visited Sonny's house in Little Italy," I say.

"You need to check out that place. There is something going on there," adds Mary Beth.

"Sonny's mom lives with him," I say.

"She doesn't know that he is dead. She still thinks he is working in Florida and staying with his friend, Franks. That is his picture there to the right. I got his picture from a friend," says Mary Beth. "Thanks to Snoop Dog."

"I found cement droppings under the dock of the Octagon house and sent it to the concrete lab for testing. The frayed rope from Sonny's leg matches the frayed rope attached to the concrete slug under the dock," says Lizzy.

"Those guys can tell the makeup of the concrete and what company uses that mixture," says Lizzy laying the report on the table. "They have traced the concrete back to a construction company in New York. I haven't had time to trace the company's owners," adds Lizzy.

"Why didn't you tell the police?" asks the agent.

"You saw Franks. We didn't trust him and figured he would find the information if he did his job," I say.

"Okay, we can have our guys find out about the construction company," Watts says.

"The day after they visited Sonny's house, Sara gets a phone call from a woman warning her to watch her back," says Lizzy looking over at me.

"Yes, I did get a call and recognized her voice as that of the union's secretary we met at the Union Hall. We were followed for a day; we had our stun guns and walked the old man's legs until he stopped following us. After we picked up the girls at the airport, we were not followed anymore," I say.

"Tony, the good-looking guy in that picture, is the president of the union and owns Carmine's restaurant. He sent wine over to our table and bought our dinner. You may want to follow the money," says Mary Beth.

"Yes, that would be prudent. Anyway, Tony had the hots for me. I played it up at the restaurant so that we could get pictures for our file," I say.

"Nancy was with us, but she immediately left the table for the restroom as soon as she saw the men heading toward us," says Elle.

"She knows nothing about our investigation unless she has opened the file I sent overnight to her house yesterday," I say. "After the men left, Nancy came back to the table and whispered in my ear, 'Those guys are suspected mobsters; Tony is the ring leader,'" I say.

"I have a question, Agent Watts. How did the men know you were coming to the farmhouse today?" I ask.

"That's a good question. I have spoken to Franks a couple of times but never met him. I did call him from my cell phone and he has access to phone tracing. That is the only way he could have known. Unless he has someone helping him in the FBI," she says. "I will find out, that is for sure," the agent adds.

Lizzy speaks up, "Until you do, we may all be in danger. The week before Cici found the body, two people were walking along the Atlantic Ocean beach near the Sea Glass House and found some large bales of pot. It looked like there were a lot of them based on the news article in the Jacksonville Journal. There is a copy in the file. The two people contacted the police right away."

"Yeah, we talked about having a bonfire if we found one of the bales," says Cici.

"Yeah, and how we would have to sleep on the beach with a bunch of munchies lying around us," says Elle.

"Okay, I will call you if I need anything. Two agents will be assigned to the front of the house and two in the back for your safety. No one knows where you other ladies live, so you should be safe," says Watts.

"How long will they be here?" asks Lizzy.

"Just a few days, I promise. I will be interrogating the two men we arrested today, and tonight I will get the information," says the agent as she rises to leave. Agent Watts picks up the file, places the timeline inside along with the pictures, and moves toward the front door. We all follow behind her. She exits the door, gets into the bureau's SUV, and rolls down her car window. "You women are amazing!" she yells back at us.

Lizzy turns, looks at us, and says, "Let's eat; I am starving."

Mary Beth and I help Lizzy gather lunch. I say, "I am going to call Weston and have him bring me some clothes. I am staying the next couple of days with you."

"I am too. I don't have any appointments and need to stay for my own mental therapy," says Mary Beth.

Lizzy pulls us together, and we all hug. "Thank you. I need my peeps right now, I don't want the kids to know," she says.

We all eat lunch, barely saying a word. The morning and afternoon excitement drained all emotions from the Beach Girls. I walk into the living room to call Weston. He picks up the phone on the first ring, which is highly unusual for him. I explain the events that had just happened.

"Baby, why don't y'all come over here and stay?" he asks.

"We will be fine staying over here with the feds. I think Lizzy will be more comfortable in her own bed tonight. Hopefully, things will get back to normal in a couple of days. Besides, Mary Beth and Lizzy have guns, and I have a cast iron frying pan," I say with a giggle. "Don't worry, baby," I add.

"You know I will," Weston replies.

"Will you bring some pairs of jeans, a few blouses from the closet, some underwear, and my brush and makeup in that little bag on the bathroom vanity?" I ask.

"You got it, babe. I will be there in a couple of hours. Do y'all need anything else?" he asks.

"No, we will be staying on the farm and hanging out," I say. "Bye. I love you," I say and hang up the phone.

Cici and Elle decide to head home, and we walk them out to Elle's car. We see the FBI agents behind the oak trees in the front yard and wave to them. The girls drive off, and we head inside the farmhouse. Weston arrives soon after with my luggage.

He gives each of us a hug and asks if he can do anything for us. Weston stays for an hour and then heads home. After a few hours of watching mindless TV shows, we all head off to bed.

Chapter Forty-One

The next afternoon, I get a call from Nancy.

"Good afternoon, frying pan girl," she says.

"How did you find out so fast?" I ask.

"Agent Watts just called me with the news. Are y'all okay?" she asks.

"Yeah, Mary Beth and I are staying at the farmhouse with Lizzy for a couple of days. Things are fine here; we haven't had any more trouble. I think it is done with," I say.

"You girls uncovered a major crime syndicate. I read your file with Rachel and my associates; we will be taking down an entire drug crime ring. Warrants are being prepared to arrest Tony and his mob this morning," says Nancy.

"Where are you? I hear a lot of talking," I ask.

"I am at the New York bureau office, DEA headquarters. The federal district attorney is moving fast on this one. Keep your eyes on the news is all I can say. Tell the girls hello," says Nancy and hangs up the phone.

After a couple of days, Lizzy sends Mary Beth and me back to our homes. "Look, I feel safe here, and you two need to get back home and back to work," says Lizzy.

"Okay, call if you need us, and keep your pistol nearby," I say.

"Okay, I just worry about you," says Mary Beth with a whimper and tears in her eyes.

For the next few weeks, the news media is flooded with arrests in New York and Florida. Tony's warrant for his arrest included drug trafficking, money laundering, tax evasion, and hiring a hit man to murder an associate. His arrest was big news across the country. Ninety-six people were arrested for drug distribution and tax evasion. Detective Franks was questioned in Florida for the attempted murder of witnesses, The Beach Girls. Mary Beth's son-in-law was made the lead on the case, and Franks doesn't have a chance of getting off. The Octagon House man was arrested for murder and conspiracy to commit additional murders.

Most of May, the Beach Girls spent with police investigators, FBI agents, DEA agents, and other agencies. The other day, two FBI agents arrive at my house. I see the black SUV in the driveway outside my front window. I open the front door, and the agent introduces himself as Agent Carter, showing me his badge.

"Sara Springs, you will have to come with us," he says.

"What are you talking about? Haven't I answered enough of your questions?" I ask.

"The grand jury in Jacksonville is in session, and you will have to testify this morning," says Agent Carter.

Luckily for me, I was dressed for school. I call the school to let them know I would not be coming in today and that they would need to have someone cover for me. Then, I grab my purse and keys and get into the SUV with the agents. Agent Carter drives twenty miles on US 1 to the federal court house in Jacksonville and parks in the police-only back lot. During the ride, the other agent hands me a bulletproof vest to put on.

"This is just routine in these kinds of cases," says Carter.

We get out of the car, and the two agents usher me up the backstairs to the grand jury's plain, tan waiting area. The room is small, with only a couple of folding chairs and a small table with a light. There are no pictures on the wall. The waiting area is kind of creepy as there are no windows and only one exit/entry. Agent Carter sits in one chair, and I sit in the other. No one says a word.

A few minutes later, the federal attorney general, Isaac Varnes, enters the room.

"Good morning Sara. I am sorry we had to take you from your job today, but under the circumstances, I thought it best if no one knew you were testifying today about the Franks attempted murder case. After the grand jury hearing today and tomorrow, I will bring charges against Franks," he says.

"It is quite all right. I am ready to get this over with and go on with my life," I say.

"Let's go," says Mr. Varnes.

We walk out of the waiting area and down a long, narrow tan hallway. The walls are lined with pictures of old and new federal judges. Even though I wanted to get this all behind me, I was still a little nervous. The Attorney-General Varnes opens the door to the small courtroom, and I walk in behind. There is a podium in the back of the room with a chair next to it and a court reporter sitting at a small desk on the other side of the podium. A long table with twelve chairs sits in front of the podium and chair. There are six men and six women seated behind the table, looking at me.

"Please state your name for the jury," says the attorney general.

"Sara Springs," I say.

"Mrs. Springs, please tell the jury your occupation," requests Mr. Varnes.

"I am a high school English teacher," I respond.

"Please explain to the jury how you know Mr. Franks," says the attorney.

"We first met a year ago at the Sea Glass House at Matanzas Beach. My friends and I were vacationing at the house and discovered a dead body at the dock. At the time, Detective Franks was the lead detective at the scene," I reply.

"Please continue with the entire story, Mrs. Springs," asks the attorney general encouragingly.

"Well," I share the entire story and then stop.

"I have a question for the witness," states juror number three, an older male.

"You may ask your question," says the attorney.

"Mrs. Springs, the way you handled the investigation is ingenious. Have you done this type of investigating before?" he asks.

"Yes, sir, my friends and I are very inquisitive and have located a few missing children and elderly adults and solved a couple of robberies. We are all amateur sleuths and enjoy solving mysteries," I answer.

"This one was very dangerous, wasn't it?" the juror asks.

"Yes. We had no idea of the magnitude of crimes and criminals involved in the murder of Sonny Manusco. Had we had any inkling, I would have hoped we would have stayed out of the investigation. I believe our investigation has helped the police, FBI, and DEA get a lot of criminals off the street. This case was solved by pure luck. If I hadn't gone to Biloxi and recognized Sonny Manusco's photo, we could not have identified him" I respond.

"I have a question?" asks juror number seven, a young woman in her early twenties.

"You may ask your question," the attorney general says.

"Mrs. Springs, what was it about Mr. Franks that made you mistrust him?" she asks.

"I guess it was his behavior when we first met. My friend Cici is an emergency room nurse; he totally dismissed her insight into what she had seen. The fact that Franks did not have anyone out in the inlet to investigate the other docks along the shoreline made no sense to me or the other ladies," I say.

Chapter Forty-Two

The following week after the federal grand jury meeting, Franks was finally arrested for the attempted murder of the Beach Girls and Agent Reynolds. James Kilroy accepted a plea deal to keep him from getting the death sentence by becoming a federal witness against the mob and Franks. Franks was turned over to the Federal Bureau of Investigation and taken to New York for a trial. The Beach Girls, after many hours and days of testimony and our case file documenting our investigation, will not have to testify in any of the cases.

The Beach Girls' next dinner is on the third Friday night in May. We decide to meet at Longhorns Restaurant out at Liberty Center at 6 pm. We arrive and the hostess seats us at a table in the back of the dining room.

"Have you ladies been watching all the news about Sonny's murder and the drug arrests?" I ask.

"Yes, that web of criminals that Tony was drug lord over was a huge ring of people. The news says his drug operation was countrywide.

According to the channel twelve news, as of last night, over two hundred people have been arrested," says Elle.

"The feds also recovered over a billion dollars in laundered money, and some of the banks out west are being investigated. They found drugs in several warehouses across the United States," says Mary Beth. "You know I never watch the news, but this week I was addicted," she adds.

"I bet they confiscated a bunch of automobiles, jewelry, and houses," says Cici. "You think they might give me one of those cars," she adds.

"Has anyone heard from Nancy?" I ask.

"She called me Wednesday night and said she has been working seven days a week since this started and is exhausted," says Cici.

"I got a call from the beach rental lady. She said we could move our vacation stay to August if we want to," says Lizzy.

"Let's do it," I say.

"Yes, that would be great!" squeals Mary Beth.

"I'm in," says Elle.

"Me, too. I'll call Nancy and let her know. I know she will go; she needs a break," says Cici as she grabs her cell phone and punches in Nancy's number.

"Hey, girl," she says.

"Hi, what's up," Nancy asks.

"We can get the Sea Glass House in August without any extra charge. Can you make it then?" asks Cici.

"Yes! That sounds wonderful. What days?" asks Nancy.

"The nineteenth through the twenty-second," says Lizzy. Cici repeats the dates to Nancy.

"Yes, I can be there. I will get my flight reservations when I hang up. Cici, you have made my day! Love you guys!" exclaims Nancy.

Chapter Forty-Three

In June, a few of us Beach Girls head to the lake house. My son owns a house right on Lake George in Palatka, Florida, and sometimes he lets us go down for a few days to relax. It is a two-story framed house with four bedrooms and three baths. It has a deck on both floors facing the water where a long dock inches out into the water. The ladies have coffee on the top deck each morning and enjoy the quietness and the morning sun.

"Look at that sun coming up just above the shoreline," says Elle.

"It is so beautiful here. No nearby houses and the views from the house are amazing. I love to see the fish jump out of the glassy, dark waters surrounding the dock," I say.

"This morning, I saw a white crane sitting on the dock," says Mary Beth.

Just then, Cici comes out on the porch, saying, "We don't have any water!"

"What do you mean we don't have any water?" I ask.

"I just put soap on my hands to wash them, and no water came out of the sink," says Cici.

Mary Beth and I get up to check the other sinks and toilets. "They were working; did you do anything?" I ask.

"No, just turned the knob to the sink," says Cici.

I call my son, and he walks me through several steps: 1. Go check the faucets outside, 2. Go check the pump to see if it is working, 3. Tell me everything you did, 4. Go switch all of the fuses in the electric box.

I do as he says and nothing.

"Okay, I will try to get a plumber out there, but it will probably be tomorrow," says Michael.

"We can make it through the night," I say.

We eat our dinner of lasagna, salad, and garlic bread, and two hours later, everyone has to go to the bathroom.

"I don't care; I am going. I can't wait," I say, rushing off to the potty.

Mary Beth yells, "Elle and I are going to the Circle K gas station to use the bathroom!"

"That gas station is over fifteen miles away!" says Lizzy.

"We can get water from the lake to put in the toilet tank," cries Cici.

"Buy some gallons of water!" I yell from the bathroom.

Mary Beth is having none of that. She grabs her keys, runs down the stairs, and off she goes with Elle to the station.

After I finish my business in the bathroom, I look for water bottles. I find some in the refrigerator, take them back to the toilet, lift the lid, and dump five bottles into the tank. I flush the toilet, and voila!

A little while later, Mary Beth and Elle return from the gas station with ten gallons of water and a case of 24 small bottles. I take two gallons to the bathroom in my room, and Lizzy takes another two to the bathroom on the main floor. Mary Beth is smiling.

After the bathroom fiasco, we turn on the TV and watch a couple of Harry Potter movies. I look over at Elle and pretend to swish a wand; she yells out, "Water."

We all laugh and continue to watch the movie.

"That should do it," says Mary Beth.

A few minutes later, Elle goes into the kitchen, forgets about the water being off, and turns on the tap.

"Water!" she yells, and we all run to the kitchen.

"I guess my magic did the trick," I say. "Check all the faucets and toilets to make sure," I add.

The girls go running throughout the house, checking for water.

"On in here!" says Lizzy.

"On in here!" the ladies yell.

"Great, I am calling Michael," I say.

I dial Michael's number. "Water's on," I say.

"That's good. The plumber couldn't come out until next Friday. I will just consider it a user error," he says, laughing.

We had no more issues the rest of our stay and still don't know what happened to the water. It is amazing what an invisible wand can do.

Chapter Forty-Four

August nineteenth arrives, and I kiss Weston goodbye. "Love you, baby," I say.

"Sara, go have a good time with your friends," says Weston. "Say hello to the Beach Girls," he adds.

I decide at the end of the school year that I will retire. It has been the best decision I have made in my professional life. Now, I will have the time to visit more with the Beach Girls. Also. I have always wanted to write a book about our investigations. Maybe, I'll start writing at the beach.

Weston loads my luggage and cooler full of frozen spaghetti sauce and two bottles of wine into the back of my SUV. Mary Beth and Lizzy are already waiting in the car. "Bye," they say to Weston.

"Have fun, y'all," yells Weston as I back the car out of the driveway.

I drive to the Oasis restaurant in St. Augustine. Cici has picked up Nancy from the airport, and they are waiting for us inside. Elle drives up and parks next to my SUV.

"I'm starving," says Elle getting out of her car. "Let's go, ladies," she adds.

We walk into the Oasis and see Cici and Nancy waving at us from a table near the restrooms.

"Hey, y'all. I got us a table near the restrooms as I figured you girls would need to go when you got here. I know I had to hurry when I got here. I drank too much water this morning," says Cici.

"I do," says Mary Beth. "I've got a bladder the size of a pea," she says, hurrying to the restroom door.

"Hello, everybody," I say. "It's finally here, the Beach Girls' weekend!" I add, doing my happy dance bouncing around and waving my hands in the air. We all hug one another.

The waitress comes to the table. "Good afternoon, ladies. May I get your drink orders," she says.

"Yes, thank you. I would like a glass of water without lemon, please," I say.

"Me, too," says Lizzy.

"I'll have an assed tea with lemon," says Cici. "You know that tea is a natural diuretic," she adds.

Nancy and Elle order Coke Zero. "I recognize you, ladies," says the waitress.

"I don't think so," I say, knowing I had never met her.

"You are the ladies that helped the feds catch that drug lord and the bad cop," she says. She leaves the table, goes into the kitchen, and returns with the New York Post newspaper. "Here, take a look," she adds.

Right on the front page of the Post is a copy of the Beach Girls photo taken at Carmine's in New York.

"How in the world did the Post get our picture?" I ask, looking straight at the girls.

Cici raises her hand and says, "I sent that picture to Nancy. I didn't know she would give it to the news media. I guess we did solve a major crime," she adds.

The waitress brings out our drinks, "You ladies are incredible," she says. The waitress sets the drinks down and goes back into the kitchen.

"Oh my gosh, this means that the news media will be hounding us," I say, exasperated.

"Not necessarily. The paper did not give our names or addresses, so if we lay low for a few days, we should be okay," says Lizzy.

"I hope so," I say.

"Don't worry, Sara," says Nancy.

The waitress returns with her manager carrying trays of food.

"Hello, ladies. This is the owner and manager of the Oasis, Bill Waters," she says.

"I just wanted to come over and let you know that your lunch is on the house. Jenny, here, showed me the article and I just had to meet you. Anyone that gets that jerk, Franks, off the street deserves a free lunch. I have had a few run-ins with him in the past, and I never liked him," says Bill. "You girls are amazing," he adds.

"Please, please don't tell anyone we are here in St. Augustine. We are trying to stay out of the limelight," says Nancy.

"You have it, ladies; I totally understand," replies Bill.

Our lunch has fried shrimp, boiled shrimp, grilled shrimp, and even shrimp scampi. It was wonderful, and we thanked the owner and the waitress. We decide to leave the waitress a big tip. She was a very sweet and efficient waitress, and we appreciate her thoughtfulness. As we walk out of the doorway, Elle yells, "I am following you, Sara, so don't drive fast!"

"I am following you too since I can't remember what road to turn on," says Cici.

"Try to keep up," I yell back.

Fifteen minutes later, driving down old US 1, we arrive at the Sea Glass House. Lizzy gets out of the SUV, grabs her keys out of the bag, and goes to open the door.

"We made it!" yells Mary Beth. "Let's get settled in," she adds.

I walk around to the back of the house and stand on the dock overlooking the Matanzas Inlet. It is so beautiful here with the sun shining on the salt water. The shimmering of the water is mesmerizing; I can barely take my eyes off it.

"Sonny, wherever you are and whatever you did in this life, I want you to know we caught your killer. Rest in peace," I say.

I go back around to the front of the Sea Glass House and help Lizzy take our luggage up to the room. We set the cases in the closet and go onto the balcony overlooking the Matanzas Inlet.

"I can't believe it has been almost a year since we discovered Sonny's body. I feel as though I knew the man," I say.

"Yeah, I know what you mean. I hope this adventure is one of fun and no dead bodies," says Lizzy.

We laugh and head downstairs to join the other girls.

"Who wants a margarita?" yells Mary Beth from the kitchen. "It's five o'clock somewhere," she adds.

We take our drinks to the dock to give Sonny a group send-off.

"Hey, Sonny, if you are still around here, you can go now," says Mary Beth.

"Listen, Sonny, I don't want any ghost hanging around me this weekend, so you need to go wherever you are supposed to go," says Cici.

"Goodbye, Sonny," says Elle.

"So long, bad guy," says Nancy.

A bright ray of sunlight chose that moment to shine down on the dock, and we backed up.

"Don't let that ray take you up to heaven. It isn't your time," says Cici grabbing me by the arm and pulling me away from the ray.

"I think the Lord knows who is to be taken," I tell Cici.

"God knows all," says Lizzy.

We head back to the Sea Glass House and decide to take our chairs to the beach. Lizzy, Mary Beth, and I place our low beach chairs at the edge of the water. I love it when the tiny waves flow across my feet. I think that I could be a mermaid if it was possible.

"This is my heaven right here on earth," I say.

"Yes, I always feel closer to God when I am at the beach like this," says Lizzy.

"Look, there are two dolphins playing in the water. See, over there," cries Mary Beth.

I look back at Elle, Nancy, and Cici and see them pointing at the dolphins. Life is good. We order pizzas for dinner and watch TV for a couple of hours. Cici brings popcorn, and I open a bottle of wine. Around twelve, we call it a night and head to our beds.

The next morning, I wake up early, nearly seven, and go to the kitchen for coffee. Cici is up and has the coffee made.

"Good morning, Sara. What you doing up so early?" she asks.

"I always get up early when I am at the beach. I like to see the sunrise. It is so magical, and I feel so at peace," I say.

"I know what you mean. I brought the orange canoe again and think I will try paddling in the Matanzas again," says Cici.

"No more bodies, please and wear your life jacket," I say. "How long will you be gone?" I ask.

"No more than an hour. Nancy and I are going out for breakfast this morning. There is a natural food diner down the road, a little piece, so we thought to try it. Want to go?" asks Cici.

"No, I'll have my fruit bar," I say.

That morning we spend the day on the beach and go for lunch at one o'clock.

"Hey, let's get a glass of wine and hang out on the pool deck for a while," I say.

While sitting on the pool deck, drinking our wine, and watching the white foam move swiftly onto the white sands of the beach, we notice a large, black SUV coming down the road.

"Not again," I say. "Can't we have one weekend of sun and relaxation," I say.

“What do the feds want now?” asks Cici.

The car pulls up to the house and steps out Agent Rachel Watts.

“Hello, ladies,” she says.

I look over at Nancy and whisper, “How did she know we were going to be here?”

“I haven’t talked to her in weeks,” she says.

“When I couldn’t reach you at home, Sara, your husband told me you were out of town for the weekend. Next, I called Nancy, and she didn’t answer her phone either. As a last hope, I called Lizzy, but no response. I remembered from the file that you ladies used a real estate agent, so I gave her a call hoping that she knew where you were. Luckily, the real estate lady told me you were all at the Sea Glass House,” says the agent.

“Dang, that woman,” I say.

“Hey, you are talking with the FBI here,” says Rachel as I roll my eyes at her. “I have something for you girls,” she says, reaching into a pocket on the inside of her jacket.

“What now, a supeenie,” cries Cici.

“Hey, if the Beach Girls don’t want it, I can keep it,” says Rachel smiling. She unfolds the check and hands it to me. I see that it is made out to Sara Springs.

“What is this?” I ask.

"The FBI could only put the check in one person's name, but it is for all of you Beach Girls. There is a three hundred thousand dollar reward for capturing your Octagon guy and for Tony's drug operation. This was a really big deal, and with all the information you ladies gave us, we had enough to go after the entire drug cartel. We are still arresting people," she says as she hands me the check.

The Beach Girls start dancing around and flapping arms as if we were a flock of geese trying to get away from a snake. I spill some of my wine on the deck, and Cici jumps up on the lounger like a lunatic and starts singing, "Oh happy day, oh happy day, when Rachel handed us that big, fat check."

"A toast, ladies," I say. "To the Beach Girls and Agent Rachel, take 'em down, girls!"

"Here, here!" yell the other girls.

"Where are we going next, ladies?" I ask.

"Las Vegas!"

Acknowledgments

I would like to acknowledge my grandchildren, Brooks, Rylan, and Caroline, who encouraged me to write and publish my books. I also want to acknowledge my husband for his support and for always telling me, "Baby, you can do whatever you want to do." Last but not least, my Beach Girls, for making my life a world of laughter and love.

About the Author

Mrs. Winters is a graduate of the University of North Florida in Jacksonville, Florida. She has a bachelor's degree in English education and a paralegal degree from the New York Paralegal Institute. Mrs. Winters is a retired English teacher and district reading coach. She has fourteen years of experience as a paralegal in a criminal law firm. Her hobbies include traveling, physical activities like zip-lining and spending time with her family. Her favorite authors are Sue Grafton, Debbie Macomber, Janet Evanovich, John Grisham, and James Patterson. As a new novelist her books are about relationships and solving mysteries with a sense of humor.

www.ingramcontent.com/pod-product-compliance
Ingram Content Group UK Ltd.
Pitfield, Milton Keynes, MK11 3LW, UK
UKHW020145250726
13967UKWH00002B/873

9 781916 787278